There's something about the Golden Gate National Recreation Area (GGNRA) you won't find in any other national park — everything.

Tucked inside these parklands of the San Francisco, San Mateo and Marin County coastal zone, you'll discover breathtaking vistas, sequestered picnic spots, backcountry campgrounds, historic landmarks, lighthouses, rare butterflies, beaches, shipwrecks, forests, and a hundred places to go and things to do. No other American national park contains such a rich blend of natural, historical and scenic features.

This guide will help you make the most of the GGNRA — whether it's learning a little-known secret about a well-known landmark or discovering new recreational frontiers on your doorstep.

Wherever your fancy takes you, the Park will bewitch you with its contrasts: old buildings with new uses, wide open spaces smack up against dense urban neighborhoods, land and water, bobcats and dairy cattle, the city and the wilderness.

Welcome to the Golden Gate National Recreation Area.

Golden Gate National Recreation Area
PARK GUIDE

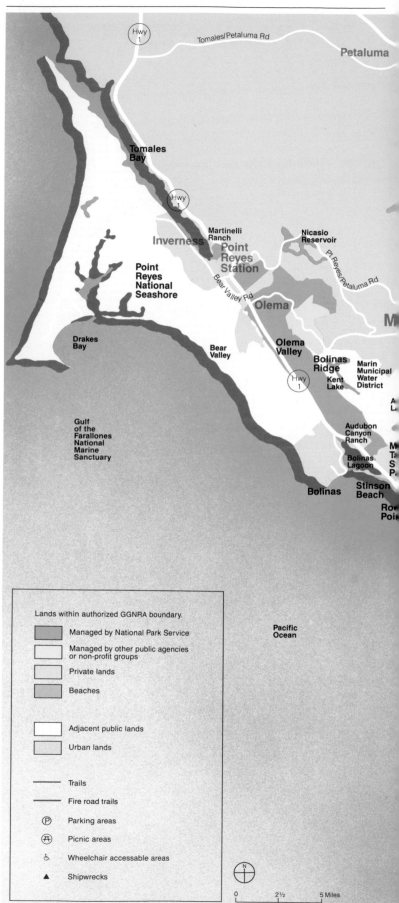

Lands within authorized GGNRA boundary.

Managed by National Park Service

Managed by other public agencies or non-profit groups

Private lands

Beaches

Adjacent public lands

Urban lands

———— Trails

———— Fire road trails

Ⓟ Parking areas

🏖 Picnic areas

♿ Wheelchair accessible areas

▲ Shipwrecks

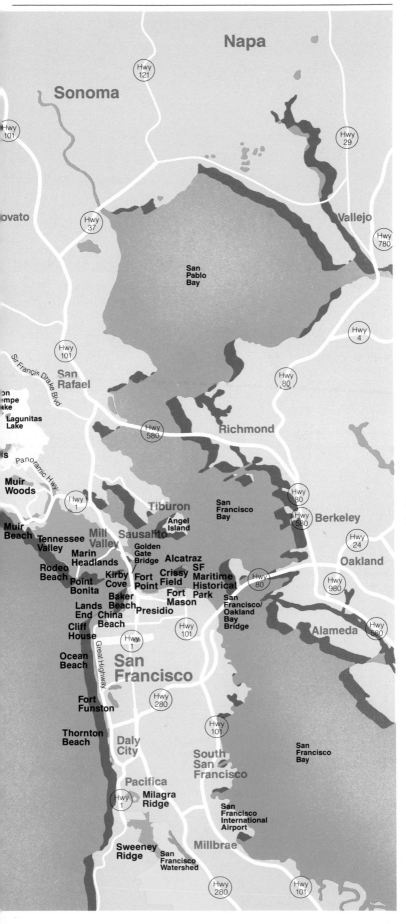

Park Highlights

To help plan your visit to the GGNRA, here's a brief overview of this remarkable national park's many features.

Spectacular Views
Every GGNRA skyline is a panorama of mountains, water, sky, and scenery. Whether it's the Bay's bridges and skyscrapers or the backcountry's golden hills and coastal cliffs, GGNRA's views are as spectacular and varied as any in the world. Favorite vista points on the San Francisco side include: Alcatraz, Fort Point, Lands End, Sutro Heights, and Sweeney Ridge. In Marin, scenic spots include East Fort Baker, Hawk Hill and Point Bonita in the Marin Headlands, and West Ridgecrest Boulevard and East Peak on Mt. Tamalpais.

Entrance Gate to Sutro Heights, ca. 1890.

Architecture
Anyone with an interest in architecture will enjoy GGNRA's diverse buildings, from the exquisite brick masonry of Civil War-era Fort Point to the steep-roofed Victorian homes of the Olema Valley. In addition, GGNRA hosts one of the nation's finest collections of military architecture. The Park's architectural highlights include: the Golden Gate Bridge, Fort Mason, Fort Point, the Presidio, the Cliff House, and the Olema Valley ranch houses.

Lighthouses
The bright beams and somber horns of three working lighthouses warn wayward ships away from GGNRA'S rocky shores. These coastal sentinels never fail to intrigue visitors with their dramatic, wind-blown locations and heroic purpose. Visitors can explore the interior of a historic lighthouse at Point Bonita, or view the 84-foot-high tower on Alcatraz — the first lighthouse ever built on the West Coast. In addition to the operational lighthouses at Alcatraz, Lime Point, and Point Bonita, the Park hosts two historic lights atop Mile Rock and Fort Point.

A Plethora of Plants
GGNRA's unusually diverse soils, microclimates, habitats, and other natural conditions enable it to sustain five different kinds of forests and over 1,000 types of plants, including 23 rare and endangered species. In the spring, wildflowers carpet the Park with purple iris, baby blue eyes, yellow sun cups, and other bright blossoms. Rare flora include the delicate lilac-flowered Mason Ceanothus and the tenacious Raven's Manzanita — a species reduced to a single remaining shrub worldwide.

Alcatraz
Alcatraz is one of GGNRA's most unusual and infamous sites, offering visitors a first-hand look at prison life, as well as fabulous bay vistas and outdoor walks around the island.

Forts and Guns

Tucked in the clifftops and crannies of the Park's rocky shore are 10 forts, over 100 gun batteries, and dozens of other facilities from all eras of American military history — one of the best preserved collections in the world. These historic seacoast fortifications tell the story of 200 years of evolving weapons technology — from the 18th century cannon to the 1970s NIKE missile. Some of GGNRA's military highlights include Fort Point, the Endicott-era batteries between the Golden Gate Bridge and Lands End, and all of the Marin Headlands.

Fort Point

Marine Life Offshore

The Gulf of the Farallones brings many oceanic wonders to GGNRA's shores, including whales, seals, dolphins, anemones, fish, birds, and other marine life. This ocean region is so rich in flora and fauna that it is protected as one of America's eight National Marine Sanctuaries.

Muir Woods

Hidden in a narrow canyon in the Park's northern heartland is one of the most famous natural areas in the world — Muir Woods. This National Monument shelters the tallest tree species known to humankind — coastal redwoods.

Shipwrecks

The Bay's elusive entrance and foggy weather have dashed many a ship against GGNRA's shores. According to maritime history records, there have been 97 shipwrecks within Park boundaries. This sunken-ship collection is both international and historical in scope, encompassing Spanish galleons, Gold Rush

schooners, and oil tankers. Famous wrecks include the *City of Rio de Janeiro* (greatest loss of life), the *Parallel* (noisiest wreck), and the *Tennessee* — a disaster which led to the construction of Point Bonita Lighthouse. During certain seasons at low tide, GGNRA visitors can actually see the water-worn remnants of shipwrecks at Lands End, Ocean Beach, and Tennessee Valley.

Hiking & Camping

Few national parks in the world offer such an extensive network of trails, fireroads, campgrounds, and hostels so near a major metropolitan area. Within a mere hour's drive lie eight camping areas, several rustic inns and rentable cabins, and hundreds of miles of trails for walks

through fern-filled canyons, over windblown coastal bluffs, along rocky shores, and among redwoods and oaks.

The Golden Gate Bridge

The world-renowned Golden Gate Bridge is the dramatic centerpiece of both the Bay Area and the GGNRA. Park visitors can walk, bike, or drive across the bridge itself, or admire it from below at Fort Point and Kirby Cove, from above at Hawk Hill in Marin, and from afar at Point Bonita and Alcatraz.

Shaky Ground

GGNRA'S location on the edge of the continent sets it firmly astride the San Andreas fault where the Pacific and North American plates have strained against each other for millennia. Bump and grind in this active fault zone have bequeathed the Park with rare rock types and soils, and other geologic wonders — many of which can be seen in the Olema Valley.

Wildlife on the Move

Over 500 species of mammals, birds, reptiles, and amphibians thrive in the Park. Bobcats bask on grassy slopes, deer dart across coastal bluffs, herons wade among lagoon grasses. In addition to year-round wildlife, myriad fauna pass through the Park on annual migrations, channeled over the GGNRA by the leading lines of north-south valleys, ridges, peninsulas, and coasts. More than 250 migrating bird species can be seen resting, nesting, feeding, and flying over the Park. Hawkwatchers have sighted as many as 2,800 migrating birds of prey on a single day.

Ranger Programs

National Park Service rangers offer a variety of interesting programs — guided walks, family activities, environmental education. A calendar of these programs is available at all visitor centers. Ranger programs include guided tours on Alcatraz, sea chantey sing-a-longs on the historic ships at Hyde Street Pier, cannonball drills at Fort Point, guided walks around the ruins of Adolph Sutro's extravagant 19th century empire, birdwatching in the Marin Headlands, and more. Call Park visitor centers for more information.

Bobcat

The Site of San Francisco in 1848

Historic Treasures

There's history everywhere you look in the GGNRA, from a 4,000-year-old Indian shellmound to the fencepost of a Gold Rush-era dairy farm. GGNRA has more National Historic Landmarks than any other unit in the National Park Service. The National Register of Historic Places lists over 700 historic sites or buildings in the GGNRA including Alcatraz, Fort Point, the San Francisco Bay Discovery Site, and the Presidio.

Alcatraz - The Cellhouse

Fort Mason Center

The GGNRA is not all nature and history. The covered piers of lower Fort Mason on the GGNRA bayfront host an exciting variety of theaters, art galleries, museums, and exhibits, as well as the offices of 50 different environmental, cultural, and recreational organizations.

Lush Wetlands

GGNRA's mudflats, marshes, lagoons and tidal flats comprise some of the wildest wetlands left in California. The abundant supply of juicy worms in the oozes, not to mention herring eggs and young fish in the water, attracts birds of every kind — land, sea, and shore. Park wetlands popular with birdwatchers include Bolinas Lagoon, Tomales Bay, and Rodeo Lagoon.

Planetary Connections

In recognition of the Park's biological riches, UNESCO recently included the GGNRA in a new Central California Coast Biosphere Reserve dedicated to the study of how humans can live in harmony with earth's life support systems. The new California reserve is the first among the world's 270 biosphere reserves to combine ocean, estuarine, and land resources in a single protected zone.

To find out more, look these Park features up in the Table of Contents (p. 3) or the Quick Glance Index (p. 95)!

Visitor Tips

Here are some tips on access to the Park, visitor safety, and preservation of the GGNRA. Please be a conscientious visitor, respectful of the beauty and fragility of this national park that belongs to us all.

■ Although wildflowers, bird nests, tidepool creatures, and other things are tempting to collect, please enjoy these wonders in their natural habitat and leave them undisturbed.

■ Trails are there to help you travel through the GGNRA and minimize erosion of its parklands. Please stick to these trails.

■ A *Park Events* calendar, available at all visitor centers, lists programs offered by the National Park Service and other Park Partners throughout the GGNRA.

■ As ocean currents off the Park's coast are dangerous, swimming is not recommended in most GGNRA waters. Also beware of tides, sneaker waves, and crumbly cliffs.

■ Visitors in wheelchairs will find accessible parking, restrooms, drinking water, and trails or buildings at areas marked on maps where this symbol appears: ♿

Other areas are partially accessible. Call 556-0560 (TDD 556-2766) for parkwide information.

■ Hikers, bicyclists, strollers, wheelchairs, cars, wildlife, and others all share Park roads and trails. Please make way for fellow travellers and observe restrictions on trail use.

■ To find out where you can mountain bike, build a fire, get drinking water, picnic, walk the dog, or ride a horse, please call Park information (see inside back cover).

■ Native flora are being carefully planted by the Park Service and volunteers. Take care not to trample young plants underfoot.

A Hot Tip for Park Lovers

There's one great way to keep in touch with the latest wildflower blooms, animal migrations, new exhibits, and other Park events, and become part of the GGNRA's preservation and care — the Golden Gate National Park Association.

The Association (GGNPA) is a nonprofit organization dedicated to the preservation, improvement, and interpretation of the Golden Gate National Recreation Area. The GGNPA keeps its members informed about the best places to go and most fascinating things to do inside the Park all year-round through an action-packed newsletter and calendar of events.

In addition, the GGNPA acts as the nonprofit support group to the National Park Service, funding vital wildlife conservation projects, spearheading new visitor programs, and organizing active volunteer efforts.

Membership applications are available at most Park visitor centers. For information contact:

 Golden Gate National
    Park Association
Fort Mason, Building 201
San Francisco, CA 94123

Membership Information:
(415) 556-2236

South of the Golden Gate

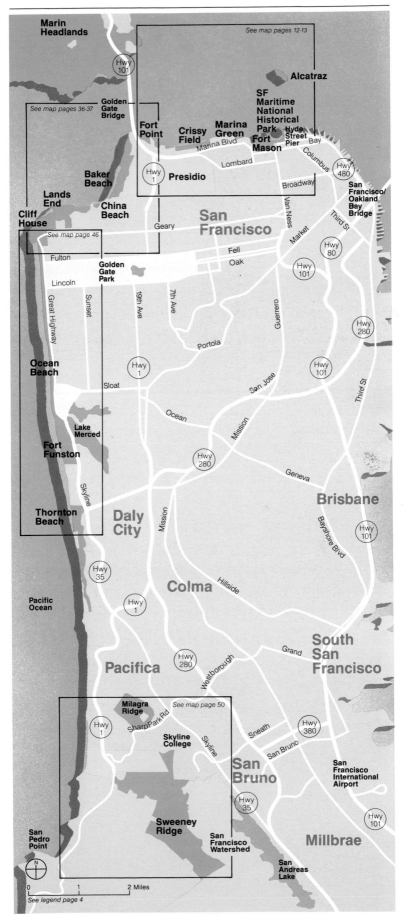

Marin
Headlands

See map pages 12-13

Hwy
101

Alcatraz

Golden
Gate
Bridge

Fort
Point

SF
Maritime
National
Historical
Park

See map pages 36-37

Crissy
Field

Marina
Green

Fort
Mason

Hyde
Street
Pier

Bay

Marina Blvd

Columbus

Hwy
480

Hwy
1

Presidio

Lombard

San
Francisco/
Oakland
Bay
Bridge

Baker
Beach

Broadway

Lands
End

China
Beach

Van Ness

Market

Cliff
House

Geary

San
Francisco

Third St.

Hwy
80

See map page 46

Fell

Fulton

Golden
Gate
Park

Oak

Hwy
101

Lincoln

Great Highway

Sunset

19th Ave

7th Ave

Guerrero

Hwy
280

Portola

Hwy
1

Ocean
Beach

Sloat

San Jose

Hwy
101

Third St

Lake
Merced

Ocean

Mission

Fort
Funston

Hwy
280

Geneva

Brisbane

Skyline

Thornton
Beach

Daly
City

Mission

Bayshore Blvd

Hwy
101

Hwy
35

Colma

Hillside

Pacific
Ocean

Hwy
1

South
San
Francisco

Grand

Hwy
280

Westborough

Pacifica

Milagra
Ridge

See map page 50

Sharp Park Rd

Skyline
College

Skyline

Sneath

Hwy
380

San Bruno

Hwy
1

San
Bruno

San
Francisco
International
Airport

Sweeney
Ridge

San Pedro
Point

San
Francisco
Watershed

Hwy
35

Hwy
101

Millbrae

San
Andreas
Lake

N

0   1   2 Miles

See legend page 4

The Bayshore

GGNRA's San Francisco Bay park-lands include Alcatraz and the scenic shoreline between Fort Mason and Fort Point — encompassing piers, seawalls, beaches, waterfront greens, and a regal brick fortress.

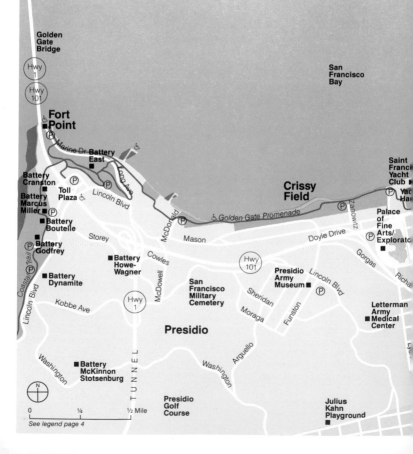

Golden
Gate
Bridge

Hwy
1

Hwy
101

**Fort
Point**

San
Francisco
Bay

Marine Dr **Battery
East**

Long Ave

**Battery
Cranston**

Toll
Plaza

Lincoln Blvd

**Battery
Marcus
Miller**

**Battery
Boutelle**

Storey

**Battery
Godfrey**

Coastal Trail

**Battery
Dynamite**

Lincoln Blvd

Kobbe Ave

**Battery
Howe-
Wagner**

Cowles

McDowell

McDonald

Mason

**Crissy
Field**

Golden Gate Promenade

Zanowitz

Saint
Franci
Yacht
Club

Yac
Har

Palace
of
Fine
Arts/
Explorato

Doyle Drive

Gorgas

Richa

Hwy
101

San
Francisco
Military
Cemetery

Sheridan

Moraga

**Presidio
Army
Museum**

Lincoln Blvd

Funston

**Letterman
Army
Medical
Center**

Hwy
1

Presidio

Arguello

Washington

Washington

**Battery
McKinnon
Stotsenburg**

TUNNEL

**Presidio
Golf
Course**

**Julius
Kahn
Playground**

N

0   ¼   ½ Mile

See legend page 4

The Golden Gate Promenade

The four-mile walk along GGNRA's Golden Gate Promenade is one of the best ways to explore the San Francisco bayshore. The promenade is a partly-paved, waterfront walkway leading from Aquatic Park to the Golden Gate Bridge. Along the promenade, visitors will find remnants of the Park's rich history including 19th-century swimming clubs, Civil War fortifications, art deco buildings, and a commercial sailing schooner. These historic sights stand against a stunning backdrop of sandy beach, waterfront green, bay water, and the Golden Gate Bridge. Any section of the promenade makes a nice walk. Joggers and bicyclists will enjoy the easy-going trail and wayside exercise stations.

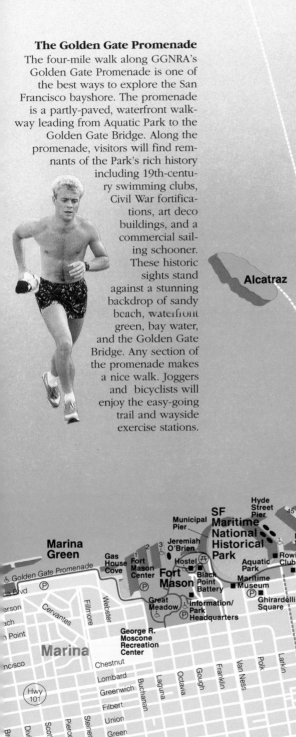

Alcatraz

Ferry to Alcatraz

Ferry to Angel Island/ Tiburon

Hyde Street Pier

45

41

Municipal Pier

SF Maritime National Historical Park

Fisherman's Wharf

43

Jefferson

Marina Green

Gas House Cove

Fort Mason Center

Jeremiah O'Brien

Hostel

Rowing Clubs

Cannery

Beach

North Point

2

3

1

Aquatic Park

Fort Mason

Black Point Battery

Maritime Museum

Columbus

Bay

Golden Gate Promenade

Great Meadow

Information/ Park Headquarters

Ghirardelli Square

Francisco

Russian Hill

Blvd

Cervantes

Fillmore

Webster

George R. Moscone Recreation Center

Russian Hill

Jones

Taylor

Mason

ncisco

n Point

Marina

Chestnut

Lombard

Greenwich

Filbert

Union

Green

Vallejo

Broadway

Pacific

Jackson

Buchanan

Laguna

Octavia

Gough

Franklin

Van Ness

Polk

Larkin

Hyde

Leavenworth

Cable Car Line

Hwy 101

Scott

Pierce

Steiner

Broderick

Divisadero

Hwy 101

Cable Car Line

Washington

Clay

Sacramento

California

Nob Hill

Alta Plaza Park

Lafayette Park

Alcatraz

Audio history tour
Island walks
Bay views
Ranger programs
Slide show
Ferry ride

Alcatraz Island is one of GGNRA's most popular destinations, offering a close-up look at a historic and infamous federal prison long off-limits to the public. Visitors to the island can not only explore the remnants of the prison, but learn about early military fortifications and the West Coast's first lighthouse. These structures stand among the island's many natural features — gardens, tidepools, bird nests, and bay views beyond compare. In addition to scenic and historical walks, Alcatraz offers a choice of activities including an audio tour of the cellhouse, ranger-led programs, and a slide show.

The Cellhouse Tour

Visitors can tour the island's imposing cellhouse with a self-guiding audio cassette (see pointers on p. 17). This award-winning audio tour tells the prison story using the actual voices of inmates and correctional officers who lived and worked on Alcatraz long ago. At that time, the cellhouse consisted of four blocks — A, B, C, and D. Each prisoner had his own cell. Prisoners who refused to follow the rules risked serving time in D-block, also known as the "Treatment Unit," where guards only let them out of isolation once a week for a brief shower and exercise period.

The worst punishment of all was a stay in "the Hole" — six, dark steel-lined boxes which deprived the senses of any stimulation.

The Lighthouse

Alcatraz is the home of the West Coast's very first lighthouse. Equipped with a simple oil lamp, the Alcatraz light began guiding ships through the narrow entrance to the Bay in 1854. In 1909, when construction of the cellhouse threatened to block the light beam to the north, the old lighthouse was replaced with an 84-foot-high tower. The tower's automated rotating light, supplemented by powerful foghorns on either side of the island, remains a key navigational aid today.

Exhibits, Theater and Bookstore

In the barracks building just above the Alcatraz ferry landing, visitors can browse exhibits and see a short historical slide show. A bookstore at this location offers maps, guides, cards, and books about Alcatraz.

View from Alcatraz

Island Walks and Bay Vistas

A walk around Alcatraz can be a breathtaking experience. The island is one of the Bay's best vista points, a place surrounded by mountains, bridges, ships, and skylines. The most spectacular views can be seen from the lighthouse plaza and the west walkway. Apart from the 360-degree panoramas of the Bay, a walk on Alcatraz takes visitors along rocky cliffs, past colonies of sea gull nests, and through areas overgrown with exotic flowers and trees.

Touring the Island with a Ranger

Rangers offer a variety of guided tours. Tour themes include natural history, San Francisco Bay, the civilian life of correctional officers, escape attempts, and other interesting topics. Look for daily tour announcements on the island's bulletin boards.

Cellhouse Information Center

An information center at the Cellhouse's front entrance offers descriptive materials, informational exhibits, and a complete selection of books, cards, posters, and videos about Alcatraz.

The Sally Port and Fort Alcatraz

The oldest standing building on the island, the Sally Port dates back to the 1850s when Alcatraz hosted the Bay's first military fort. Walking through this early guardhouse, it is easy to imagine the impressive drawbridge that once spanned the building's dry moat. At the dock below the Sally Port, visitors will find the fort's original barracks. Built for soldiers and cannon, the fortified foundations of

the barracks now house displays, a bookstore, and a theater. Other relics of the island's military past include an overgrown parade ground, the ruins of officers' cottages, and the first floor of the original military citadel on Alcatraz. This maze of rooms now serves as a foundation for the cellhouse.

From Fort to Park : History of Alcatraz

Fort Alcatraz
1859-1907

Alcatraz guarded the strait of San Francisco Bay between 1859 and 1907, serving as the Bay's only defense until Fort Point (see p. 28) was completed in 1861. Alcatraz's fortifications and firepower included more than 100 cannon.

The Military Prison
1861-1933

Alcatraz's first inmates weren't bank robbers or thugs but Confederate sympathizers, disobedient soldiers, Indians, and suspected war spies. Fort Alcatraz was converted into a permanent military prison in 1907.

The Federal
Penitentiary
1934-1963

When crime swept America during Prohibition and the Great Depression, the federal government responded by building a new form of prison for the most incor-

rigible public enemies and troublemakers. The maximum-security, minimum-privilege Alcatraz facility was specially designed to discipline criminals so troublesome that other federal prisons couldn't handle them. Alcatraz kept an average of 264 inmates behind bars during its 29 years of operation. Due to the difficulties and expense of operating such an isolated facility, Alcatraz closed in 1963.

Native
American
Occupation
1969-1971

While Alcatraz stood empty and the federal government debated its fate, a

boatload of 89 Native Americans claimed the island as "Indian land." For two years, the group tried to establish a Native American educational and spiritual center. Frustrated by lack of support and personal tragedies, and confronted by U.S. Marshalls, the Native Americans left Alcatraz in 1971.

A Public Park
1973 —

Alcatraz reopened to the public in 1973 as part of the GGNRA, offering visitors a unique, first-hand experience of the island. The National Park Service is still working to enhance access to Alcatraz by

developing new walkways, clearing rubble, nurturing plant and animal communities, and improving exhibits and visitor programs.

The Gardens of Alcatraz

Military and prison personnel transformed Alcatraz from a barren rough rock to an island of lush leaves and colorful blossoms. Undaunted by the exposed hostile conditions, the people of Alcatraz chipped away

at the rock, imported topsoil from nearby Angel Island, and planted flowers, vegetables, trees, and other greenery. In prison times, digging around in the front and backyard became so popular that guards and their fami-

lies formed a special gardening association. After years of neglect, the gardens outgrew their plots and ran wild, presenting today's visitors with a host of plant varieties no longer available from nurseries.

Bird Life

Over the years, Alcatraz's isolation has not only made it a desirable location for a prison, but also for wildlife. The island's secluded, predator-free conditions attract hundreds of gulls and other birds. It's one of the largest Western Gull nesting sites on the West Coast. In addition to the gulls, Black-crowned Night Herons nest on Alcatraz. The gulls are easily visible on the west side of the island; the herons often hide in the bushes along the walkway between the bar-racks/bookstore build-ing and the cellhouse.

Black-crowned Night Heron
Body Color: White breast/grey back
Head Color: Grey/black and long white plume
Bill: Black
Size: Very Large
Occurrence: Year-round

Western Gull
Body Color: White body/grey wings
Head Color: White
Bill: Yellow
Size: Large
Occurrence: Year-round

Notorious Inmates

Al "Scarface" Capone
Convicted of tax evasion, gangster Al Capone stayed five years on Alcatraz, one of the many Depression-era "public enemies" imprisoned on the island.

Alvin "Creepy" Karpis
Kidnapper Karpis was the FBI's Public Enemy No. One in 1936. Many inmates described him as a creepy "weasel" and "wimp." After 27 years and nine months on Alcatraz, longer than any other inmate, Karpis was transferred and eventually paroled.

Robert Stroud "The Birdman"
Stroud was an Alaskan Gold Rush pimp and two-time murderer. While at Leavenworth prison, he kept birds and wrote a book on bird diseases. Stroud spent 54 years of his life behind bars, 17 on Alcatraz, where he was not allowed to keep birds.

Pointers

◆ Transportation to Alcatraz is via ferry-boats, departing from Pier 41 at Fisherman's Wharf. The ferry trip lasts ten minutes. A round-trip visit takes between two and three hours. Reser-vations are essential in the busy summer season. Tickets can be purchased in advance at any Ticketron out-let or at Pier 41, or by phone with a major credit card through Teletron.

◆ Self-guiding audio cas-settes are available at the cellhouse en-trance for a nominal fee.

◆ Don't miss the self-guiding, information-packed *Official Map and Guide to Alcatraz*, available from all Park book-stores.

◆ Dress warmly. Alcatraz lies directly in the path of freezing wind and fog sweeping through the Golden Gate.

◆ Be prepared for steep climbs.

◆ The island's limited supply of drinking water is only available at the ranger office on the dock.

◆ Toilets are located on the dock and near the cellhouse's entrance.

Information: 556-0560
Ferry information: 546-2805
Teletron: 392-7469

San Francisco Maritime National Historical Park

Museum exploring
Historic ship tours
Maritime history
Photo research
Swimming
Fishing
Picnicking

T he San Francisco Maritime National Historical Park takes visitors on a trip through the West Coast's colorful seafaring past. From a 450-ton lumber schooner to a ship in a bottle, the park brings together one of the finest collections of historic ships, models, photographs, and maritime artifacts in the world. For years, this collection was part of the GGNRA. In 1988, however, it became a national park in its own right. This historic area is located in Aquatic Park, a bayshore cove where San Franciscans have been coming to swim, row, fish, and enjoy the waterfront for over a century.

The Exhibits

The white oval Maritime Museum building at Aquatic Park houses most of the maritime park's indoor exhibits. The exhibits span more than a century of West Coast seafaring history, beginning in the 1840s. Ground-floor displays include intricate models of famous vessels, name boards, and figureheads; one room is devoted entirely to steamships. The exhibits upstairs bring to life the men and women who built, supplied, and sailed the Gold Rush ships and Cape Horners, as well as local whalers, yachts, and ferry boats. Check for current exhibit and special events information. Outdoor displays include the unique flotilla of historic ships at Hyde Street Pier along the Aquatic Park waterfront. The pier gives kids and adults alike the chance to see and explore actual vessels such as the majestic schooner *C.A. Thayer* and the hundred-year-old ferryboat *Eureka* (see pp. 20-21).

Hyde Street Pier

The Waterfront

Aquatic Park's beach, benches, and vista points invite visitors to enjoy the waterfront scenery. The park makes an excellent starting point for a bayside walk, jog, or bike along the Golden Gate Promenade and through GGNRA's adjacent parklands. The 185-foot pier offers fishing and views of the city's northern waterfront architecture, Alcatraz, and the Golden Gate Bridge.

Historic Documents and Library

The J. Porter Shaw Library and Historic Documents Department, located at lower Fort Mason, have more than 12,000 volumes on maritime subjects, as well as an extensive collection of oral history interviews, periodicals, log books, maritime archives, and ship plans — more than 100,000 sheets of plans, in fact. In addition, the library houses a collection of more than 250,000 historic photographs of Pacific Coast maritime activities and early San Francisco, as well as of ships, ports, and seafarers from all over the world.

Art and Architecture

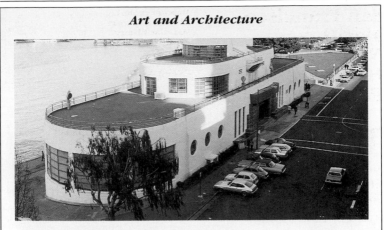

Despite the marble, chrome, sculpture, and extravagant architecture, Aquatic Park wasn't built for the rich. This 1930s waterfront park with a nautical design theme was built for the people of San Francisco by the Depression-era Works Progress Administration (WPA). For the park's facilities, architect William A. Moser III chose a Streamlined Moderne style inspired by the dynamics of airplanes, trains, and ships — a style also known as the "giant appliance" approach. The park's centerpiece is a palatial bathhouse in the form of a luxury ocean liner, complete with stainless steel railings, portholes, and decks. Today, the bathhouse serves as the home of a maritime museum. The museum building, as well as most of Aquatic Park's other WPA-era structures, are now listed in the National Register of Historic Places.

Visitor Programs

The National Park Service offers a variety of ranger-led walks and talks around the historic ships, including an engine room tour of the impressive ferryboat *Eureka*. Special programs range from sea chantey sing-a-longs to maritime history movies. Volunteers are invited to help with ship restoration work.

Famous escape artist Harry Houdini unshackled himself from chains underwater at Aquatic Park in 1907.

The Maritime Store

The store at Hyde Street Pier sells items with a maritime twist, offering books, posters, cards, and gifts with themes ranging from lighthouses and sea chanteys to shipbuilding.

Pointers

◆ Visitors can board the Powell-Hyde cable car at Aquatic Park and take a scenic and breezy trip to Union Square. Be prepared to line up during the tourist season.

◆ Swimmers will find the water warmest in September. Temperatures range from 51 to 60 degrees Fahrenheit. Lockers and showers are available under the bleachers. Lifeguards are on duty in the summer.

◆ Take the bus to Aquatic Park whenever possible. Parking is difficult.

◆ The public can anchor boats in Aquatic Park lagoon for 24 hours.

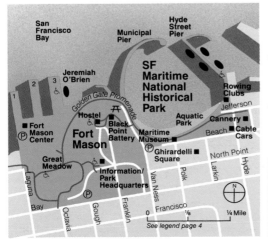

See legend page 4

Information:

S.F. Maritime National Historical Park: 556-3002

Library: 556-9870

Maritime Store: 775-2665

The Ships

The San Francisco Maritime National Historical Park manages the largest collection of historic ships by tonnage in the world. The best place to begin exploring the collection is at Hyde Street Pier, mooring place of a square-rigger, schooner, ferry, and other historic vessels (a nominal admission fee is charged). The rest of the collection can be found at other bayfront access points.

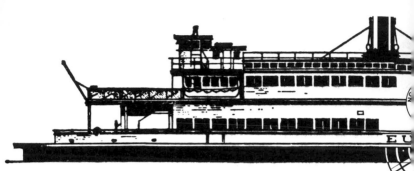

C.A. Thayer

Type: Three-masted "bald headed" schooner
Location: Hyde Street Pier
Built: Fairhaven, California, 1895
Length: 156 feet
Gross Tonnage: 452

In her early days, *C.A. Thayer* undertook the dangerous business of picking up lumber along California's rugged coast and delivering it to San Francisco and ports across the Pacific. She later participated in the Alaskan salmon trade and worked as a codfishing vessel in the Bering Sea. *C.A. Thayer* was the last commercial sailing vessel to operate from a western U.S. port.

"Life on a Pacific Coast lumber schooner was not so bad, and the fo'c'sle in most of them was snug and dry.... It was kind of eerie when reefing down in a rising gale, the schooner heeling way over, the water rushing along and lapping over the top of the deckload to lee. But everybody knew his work, and it was done in no time at all."

Captain Fred K. Klebingat

Hercules

Type: Ocean-going steam tug
Location: Pier 1, Fort Mason (temporary berth)
Built: New Jersey, 1907
Length: 135 feet
Gross Tonnage: 414

Hercules was a high-powered tugboat with a 1,000-horsepower steam engine. Built on the East Coast, *Hercules* went west to break up

the tugboat monopoly in San Francisco Bay, making the hazardous journey through the Straits of Magellan unscathed. In her time, *Hercules* proved worthy of her name. She built a piece of the Panama Canal, hauled log rafts down the West Coast to lumber mills, and towed great sailing vessels and warships out to sea.

"We picked up six million feet of timber in a raft to tow to San Diego. Long, slow, lazy days, making no more than three knots, even the patent log wouldn't work. We rigged a fishing line on it and caught beautiful king salmon on the way."
Albert Hody, *Hercules* Fireman

Alma

Type: Scow schooner
Location: Hyde Street Pier
Built: San Francisco, California, 1891
Length: 59 feet
Gross Tonnage: 42

Alma is the last of a stocky breed of flat-bottomed sailing boats built to navigate the shallow waters of San Francisco Bay. *Alma* never ventured beyond inland waters, but she traveled back and forth across the Bay with loads of hay, brick, lumber, and later, oyster shells. The crew often piled the cargo so high the steering wheel had to be raised up so the helmsman could see where he was going. Restored to her original splendor, *Alma* still sails today.

"The Bay used to be full of them...those scow schooners with their stove pipes and their loads of hay...a sciving around and goin' it...or waiting to get in on the tide."

F.H. Warde

Eureka

Type: Double-ended side-wheel ferryboat
Location: Hyde Street Pier
Built: Tiburon, California, 1890
Length: 300 feet
Gross Tonnage: 2,564

The ferryboat *Eureka* began her days as a railroad car ferry called *Ukiah*. In 1922, she was rebuilt to take commuters and their automobiles across the Bay as *Eureka*. She was the world's largest passenger ferry in her day, with a four-story-high steam engine and a deck the length of a football field. *Eureka* could carry 2,300 passengers and 120 cars from San Francisco to Sausalito in 27 minutes.

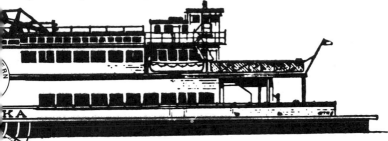

Balclutha

Type: Square-rigged sailing ship
Location: Hyde Street Pier
Built: Scotland, 1886
Length: 256
Gross Tonnage: 1,716

Balclutha is one of the last great 19th-century sailing ships. During her first years at sea, she rounded Cape Horn 17 times bringing coal, wine, and wool from Europe, and returning with California grain. Later, *Balclutha* made San Francisco her home port and joined the Alaska Packers fleet. Under the new name of *Star of Alaska*, she carried fishermen north in pursuit of the "great silver horde."

"Everyone is anxious to get into port after a long voyage. One might meet a relative or dear friend, and get a change of food from salt meat and canned goods to fresh meat and vegetables! Also to have grass to walk on after the wooden decks was all very enticing!"
Alfred H. Durkee, *Balclutha* Captain

Eppleton Hall

Type: Paddletug
Location: Hyde Street Pier
Built: England, 1914
Length: 100 feet
Gross Tonnage: 106

Eppleton Hall came from England. She's a close relation of the simpler paddletugs with sidewheel steam engines once used to tow clipper ships on the Bay.

Wapama

Wapama

Type: Steam schooner
Location: Army Corps of Engineers dock, Sausalito
Built: St. Helens, Oregon, 1915
Length: 216 feet
Gross Tonnage: 951

Designed specifically for easy maneuvering along the rocky shoreline, *Wapama* survived 15 years of rugged work, hauling lumber through fog and across heavy seas. After 65 years as a lumber carrier, passenger vessel, freighter, and museum vessel, this great wooden steam schooner was dry-docked for preservation work.

"Great grub, fine pay, but work to kill you."
Wapama Crew Member

Jeremiah O'Brien

Type: Liberty Ship
Location: Pier 3, Lower Fort Mason
Built: South Portland, Maine, 1943
Length: 441 feet
Displacement Tonnage: 7,500

During World War II, German submarines were sinking Allied ships by the hundreds. Cargo ships were so hard to come by that President Franklin D. Roosevelt ordered production of a fleet of "Liberty" ships. In a mammoth national effort, 48 shipyards in 21 states, operating around the clock, managed to lay three keels and launch one ship a day. The Liberty ships carried beans, bullets, and toilet paper. During the D-Day build-up, *Jeremiah O'Brien* made 11 supply shuttles and even ferried part of General Patton's Fifth Infantry Division to Normandy.

"Admiral, I think this ship will do us very well. She'll carry a good load. She isn't much to look at, though, is she? A real ugly duckling."
President Franklin D. Roosevelt

Fort Mason

Visitor information
Walking
Picnicking
Cultural center
Fishing
Youth hostel

Fort Mason occupies the northernmost point of land in San Francisco. This bayfront promontory has attracted people throughout California history, from Spanish soldiers to the American army, from earthquake refugees to port authorities. Today, one historic military building at upper Fort Mason serves as GGNRA headquarters, another as a youth hostel. Down by the water, lower Fort Mason's piers and warehouses host the Fort Mason Center and its dynamic variety of cultural, environmental, and recreational activities. Shady trails and steep stairs traverse the slope between upper and lower Fort Mason, giving access to Black Point Battery, the Great Meadow, and Aquatic Park.

Fort Mason Center

The covered piers and warehouses at lower Fort Mason provide space for 50 different environmental, theatrical, artistic, and musical organizations. The Center is managed by the Fort Mason Foundation, a nonprofit organization established in 1977.

Visitors to the Center will find art galleries, ethnic museums, theaters, a dance coalition, a restaurant, and organizations such as Greenpeace and the Media Alliance. In addition to its regular tenants, more than 500 different groups use the Center's facilities on a monthly basis for special events and programs ranging

from workshops on Japanese mime to the Firefighters' Chili Cookoff. For more information, pick up the Center's monthly schedule of activities from lobby areas.

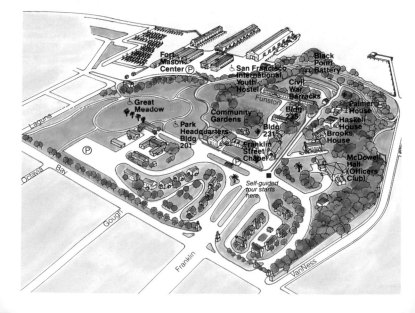

Park Headquarters

One good place to begin exploring GGNRA is Park Headquarters, which is housed in a gracious, white, three-story building at upper Fort Mason. The headquarters can also provide information on other western national parks.

Fort Mason and the Great Meadow

The Great Meadow

A large lawn slopes down from upper Fort Mason to the Marina, offering grassy hilltops and hollows for picnicking, sunbathing, walking, or sports. Views from the meadow include San Francisco's hilly skyline and the Golden Gate Bridge.

Earthquake Refugees

After the famous jolt of 1906, the tents of earthquake refugees dotted Fort Mason's Great Meadow. While the city collapsed and burned, thousands of hungry and homeless people received care at Fort Mason — headquarters for army relief field operations.

Port of Embarkation

Lower Fort Mason was the nerve center of wartime embarkation programs between 1910 and 1963. Thousands of men and tons of supplies passed through the facility's three deep-water finger piers on their way to war zones across the ocean.

Black Point Battery and Picnic Area

When the Civil War broke out in the East, San Francisco's coastal defense rested solely on the firepower of Fort Point and Alcatraz. The Union valued California's natural resources and built three emergency fortifications in the Bay Area, including Black Point Battery, to protect them. Six 10-inch Rodman cannon (weighing 24,000 pounds each) and an equal number of smaller "James" guns armed the battery, but not one of these weapons ever fired a shot at the Confederates. Named for the dark cluster of laurel trees which once grew on the bluff, Black Point Battery is the only intact temporary Civil War fortification west of the Rockies. Here, visitors will find a sheltered picnicking and sunbathing spot overlooking the battery and the Bay.

East of the piers, visitors will find the only unaltered stretch of bay shoreline left in the City.

Pointers

- Don't miss the *Jeremiah O'Brien* at Pier 3 (see p. 21).
- Lower Fort Mason has two places to get food: Greens in Building A, a restaurant featuring elegant vegetarian dining; and Cooks & Co. in Building B, offering take-out food and drink.

- For information on the San Francisco Youth Hostel at Fort Mason, see p. 69.
- The Park Police headquarters is at upper Fort Mason.

Information:
Park Headquarters: 556-0560
Fort Mason Center: 441-5705

A Self-Guided Tour of Fort Mason

A walk through Fort Mason, a National Historic Landmark, offers an interesting tour of many eras of military architecture and history. Follow the route marked on the map on page 22 and read other sections on these pages for more information on historic structures.

● Begin at upper Fort Mason with a look at the Black Point wayside exhibit just north of the Chapel on Franklin Street. Look east across the lawn to **McDowell Hall** — the Officers' Club and former home

McDowell Hall in 1939

of a succession of commanding officers. This regal green building, flanked by palms, eucalyptus, and pine, was largely built by General McDowell in 1877. Over the years, two Presidents and countless dignitaries have been wined and dined at McDowell Hall.

● Walk north towards San Francisco Bay along Franklin. To the right stand three stately frame houses — the **Brooks, Haskell,** and **Palmer** houses — built during the Gold Rush by wealthy San Francisco businessmen. These elegant Greek Revival-style homes date back to the days before Fort Mason became a military reserve. Military families live in them today.

● Continue along Franklin and down the steps to the picnic area and **Black Point Battery** (see p. 23). The

battery's breast-high brick walls housed Civil War cannon and guns. As the battery curves to an end, turn left on Magazine Road and walk around to the front of the **San Francisco International Youth Hostel.** The hostel building was originally built as barracks for Civil War soldiers.

● Walk down Funston Street and turn right on Franklin. Along the right side of Franklin stand several interesting buildings: **Building 235**, the former headquarters and residence of the commanding officer of the military post at Fort Mason; and **Building 231**, a charming officer's house built in the 1880s with a steep red roof and circular window frame.

● Just west of the Mission Revival-style **Chapel** at the corner lies the largest building at Fort Mason — **Park Headquarters.** This much-remodeled building served as a military post hospital and later as headquarters for San Francisco's Port of Embarkation. Long ago, the tiny structure across the street sheltered streetcar riders from the brisk Pacific winds.

● Sloping down from the headquarters building lies the green expanse of the **Great**

Meadow — home of earthquake refugees and support facilities for Fort Mason's piers (see p. 23).

● Following the edge of the Great Meadow around the corner of Park Headquarters, look over the fertile **community gardens** full of bright blossoms and juicy vegetables. Gardens have flourished on this site since military families planted the first seeds in the 1860s.

● Walk along the edge of the Meadow and down the stairs marked **"Piers."** The red-tiled roofs, white stucco facades, and solid lines of lower Fort Mason's piers and warehouses evoke the Spanish Colonial style of architecture on a grand, yet simple, scale. This former port of embarkation, built between 1910 and 1940, today serves as the home of the Fort Mason Center.

Marina Green

**Jogging
Kite flying
Bicycling
Strolling
Volleyball
Sunbathing**

I f San Francisco were one big household, Marina Green would be its front yard. Marina Green's acres of lawn are surrounded by grand homes, bay vistas, and white yachts. Though owned by the City of San Francisco, Marina Green provides an easily accessible bridge between GGNRA parklands on either side.

The Green

Marina Green is one of the flattest, windiest, and most accessible open spaces in San Francisco. There's no better place to fly a kite than this vast lawn unobstructed by trees or buildings. The sheltered pocket of grass down by the yacht club, "Little Marina Green," lends itself to volleyball and summer sunbathing.

The Waterfront Promenade

For strollers, cyclists, and sailboat enthusiasts, the Golden Gate Promenade paves the way from Fort Mason to Crissy Field along the Marina.

The Fitness Parcourse

Parcourse fitness stations on Marina Green invite visitors to do a few sit-ups and leg-lifts or swing from the parallel bars.

The Outer Seawall

The seawall extending out from the St. Francis Yacht Club is a terrific place for bayside strolling and front-row views of yacht racing (particularly on a flood tide). At the end of the seawall is a rather unusual attraction, a wave organ where visitors can listen to the sounds of the Bay through pipes sunk into the water.

Panama Pacific International Exposition

San Francisco put itself back together with such spirit after the 1906 earthquake and fire that President Taft chose it as the city to host the Panama Canal opening celebration. The

Panama Pacific International Exposition of 1915 filled 635 acres of the Marina District with palaces, festival halls, race tracks, amusements, and pavilions. One of the most lavish exposition buildings — the Palace of Fine Arts — still graces the view from Marina Green today.

Pointers

◆ Bring a windbreaker.

The Palace of Fine Arts

> **Information:**
>
> **SF Recreation & Parks:
> 666-7200**

Crissy Field

Walking
Birdwatching
Beachcombing
Jogging
Windsurfing
Fishing

At first glance, Crissy Field looks like a jumble of military buildings at the west end of Marina Green. But visitors who venture along this historic airfield will discover a veritable urban wilderness with a sizable beach, a variety of sea and shorebirds, and unobstructed bay views. Long ago, the natural features of this semi-wild stretch of bayfront land included a bank of sand dunes and a lush salt marsh. Today, Crissy Field is not only a favorite spot for walking, jogging, and picnicking, but also a nationally renowned windsurfing site.

Windsurfing

Crissy Field is one of the most popular and challenging windsurfing sites in the world. The bay winds blow strongly offshore, and the beach affords easy access to the water. The most active windsurfing period is between March and October.

The Dunes

The sand dunes flanking Crissy Field's beach were once part of a vast dune field edged by salt marshes and lagoons. These small mountains of sand are the only dunes on the GGNRA bayfront where native dune grass still grows. In an effort to restore Crissy's historic vegetation, the Park Service is planting more of the native *Elymus mollis* — a thick, green grass hardy enough to withstand the strong west wind, cool fog, and airborne sand.

The Beach

Crissy's beach brings visitors right to the water's edge. These sandy parklands comprise the longest, wildest, and most pristine beach on San Francisco's northern coast.

The Golden Gate Promenade

For joggers and walkers who prefer pavement to the uneven beach terrain, the Golden Gate Promenade slices through Crissy Field on its way from Marina Green to Fort Point.

Crissy's Historic Airfield

An overgrown clearing, a row of hangars, and a slimy seaplane ramp evoke the time when a squadron of airplanes stood ready for action at Crissy Field. This military airfield is actually older than the Air Force, dating back to the 1920s when flying had barely gotten off the ground. In those days, so little was known about nationwide flying conditions that the U.S. Army sent a team of fliers up from Crissy Field and an eastern counterpart at the same time to see who could reach the opposite coast first. In the absence of any real enemy, Crissy's squadron (the 91st Aero) flew forest-fire patrols, spotted for seacoast fortifications, and took aerial photos. Crissy was also used for the first coast-to-coast transcontinental flight to be completed between dawn and dusk.

Crissy Field, ca. 1930

A Visit from the HMS Racoon

During the War of 1812, Great Britain sent the HMS *Racoon* to the West Coast to take possession of the American fur trading post at Astoria, Oregon. Drawings and entries in the ship's journal describe hauling the *Racoon* out on Crissy Field's beach to repair holes in the bow so big the seamen were shocked they'd made it into port, let alone halfway around the world. The author of one journal entry describes in olde English the San Francisco of more than a century ago: "The Country abounds in all kinds of Wild Beasts, Bears, Wolves, Mountain Cats....which are at times of Young exceeding ferocious and destroys a number of the Indians.... [they] never attacked any of us, except one Man, in the woods, cutting plank to repair the Ship's Bottom; and he was devoured. They also have [a] great abundance of seals on their coast, but they make no manner of use of them; and they, like lawless animals, rove free and uncontroled through the wilds of love."

Dungeness Crabs

Dungeness crabs use the Bay as a nursery. Born in the ocean, many millions of crab larvae migrate and drift into the Bay. The larvae grow into young crabs in food-rich shoreline areas such as the waters off Crissy Field. As these orange crabs with white claws don't reach maturity until long after returning to the ocean, it's illegal to trap them in the Bay.

Pointers

♦ Crissy is particularly nice for quiet morning walks before the wind picks up.

♦ The best time to see the beach at its widest is at low tide.

♦ Fishermen will find a pier at the west end of Crissy Field.

Information:
556-0560

Fort Point

Fort tours
Exhibits
Cannonball drills
Walking
Surfing

Though dwarfed by the Golden Gate Bridge today, Fort Point's four tiers of cannon were once the most awesome feature at the entrance to San Francisco Bay. This mighty fort kept an unerring vigil over the golden gateway for more than a century, but no enemy ever challenged its might. Today, Fort Point is a National Historic Site. Visitors can explore its brick casemates, marvel at its grand arches and spiral stairs, participate in one of the daily cannon drills, or join a tour at the bugle call.

Fort Tours and Cannon Drills

Rangers clad in full Civil War uniform lead frequent tours of the fort, but visitors may also walk around on their own. On the ground floor, visitors can see a soldier's jail cell, examine an array of historic cannon, walk into a powder magazine, and browse a number of special exhibits on the fort's colorful history. The second floor includes the officers' quarters, kitchen, and hospital rooms. The third floor houses the soldiers' barracks. Those who find their way to Fort Point's fourth floor, the "barbette tier," will be rewarded with an unparalleled view of the Bay's entranceway from directly under the Golden Gate Bridge. After exploring the fort, don't miss a chance to load a smoothbore cannon during one of the drills.

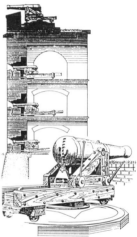

Trails

Fort Point visitors can chose from a number of trails affording hillside walks and coastal hikes.

Fort Point Loop

Features: Golden Gate, Fort Point, San Francisco views

Access: Take the winding hillside trail up toward the Golden Gate Bridge toll plaza from the Fort Point parking lot. Bear right when the road forks near the top and walk up through the flagpole plateau. Continue down the other side of the plateau and follow the trail left. Pass the Joseph B. Strauss statue and bear right at the memorial plaque, and right again on the first cement trail. Follow the trail through the picnic area, past Battery East, and back down to Fort Point.

Round trip: Less than 1 mile

Coastal Trail

Features: Coastal views, wildflowers, sea-coast fortifications

Access: Take the hillside trail up from the Fort Point parking lot. Go under the bridge and follow the hiker's signs along the San Francisco Headlands to Lands End and beyond.

One way: To Fort Funston, 12 miles

The Origins of Fort Point

During the War of 1812, the British landed in Chesapeake Bay and marched straight into the nation's capital. Embarrassed by this demonstration of America's weak coastal defenses, President Madison ordered a new system of permanent forts to guard the nation's seaport cities. Completed in 1861 at a cost of $2.8 million, Fort Point was the only one of these "Third System" forts built on the Pacific Coast.

Fort Point's Active Duty

During the Civil War, 140 men manned Fort Point, equipped with 90 heavy artillery pieces, two flank casemate howitzers, and five coehorn mortars. The fort never fired a shot, however; the Confederates never dared to attack. If they had, the fort's walls could have theoretically withstood the impact of 10,000 cannonballs before giving way. After the Civil War, Fort Point was intermittently garrisoned. It wasn't long before the invention of rifled cannons capable of breaching brick walls made the structure obsolete. Fort Point saw its last active duty in World War II.

Ranger William F. Wolper

The Sutler's Store

The sutler's store at Fort Point sells belt buckles, blankets, bullets, and other essentials that a Civil War soldier might have purchased from the sutler — a civilian merchant at an army post — as well as an array of American history publications, postcards, and color slides.

Pointers

◆ The fort can be extremely cold and windy any day of the year, so dress warmly.

Information:
556-1693

The Presidio

S ince the first Spanish garrison arrived in 1776, the Presidio's soldiers have never let up their guard over the riches of San Francisco Bay. This serene corner of San Francisco comprises both the oldest continuously-used military post in the nation, and the most beautiful. Within the legislated boundaries of the GGNRA, Presidio lands and buildings are gradually being transferred from the Army to the National Park Service. As both an open post and national park, the Presidio offers forests, creeks, trails, views, architecture, and history for today's Park visitors.

Presidio Army Museum

Any tour of the Presidio should begin at the Army Museum, where visitors can learn about the history of this venerable military post, examine various Army uniforms and equipment, and trace the special experiences of Blacks, women, and Japanese-Americans at war. The museum also hosts intriguing dioramas depicting the marvels of the 1915 Panama Pacific Exposition and the 1939 World's Fair.

Presidio Coat of Arms

Forests of the Presidio

The Presidio's tall, dark, handsome forests were not always a fixture of the local landscape. Early soldiers complained of the harsh sand, rock, and grass of the post's hills and hollows. The grim setting inspired Major Jones of the Army Corps of

Engineers to prepare a tree-filled landscape plan for the Presidio in 1883. Scattered seedlings soon grew into strapping forests — 60,000 trees were planted in the 1880s alone. As a result, Presidio visitors will see an extraordinary variety of trees, among them acacia, cypress, eucalyptus, madrone, redwood, spruce, and the exotic Portuguese cork oak. There are at least 30 different types of trees along the Ecology Trail alone (see map below).

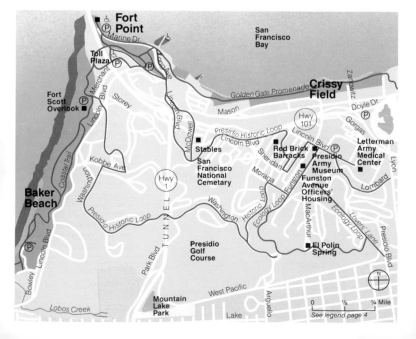

Historic Landmarks and Architecture

The Presidio is an unparalleled showcase of military landmarks and architectural history. The post and its hundreds of historic buildings received National Historic Landmark status in 1963. Points of interest include:

Officers' Club

Built on the foundations of the original Spanish "Commandancia" (headquarters), the present day Officers' Club is a graceful Spanish Colonial Revival-style building on Moraga Avenue. Inside, visitors can see a portion of the original adobe wall that Spanish Commander Jose Moraga erected around his compound in 1776.

Red Brick Barracks

Built in the Georgian style between 1895 and 1897, the regal, brick barracks flanking the Parade Ground off Montgomery Avenue served as the enlisted men's first permanent barracks at the Presidio.

Presidio soldiers on patrol in Yosemite, ca. 1899.

Stables

The old, brick stables on McDowell Avenue, now used for storage and automobile repair, recall the time when the Army conducted its maneuvers on horseback. Mounted Presidio soldiers patrolled not only the Pacific coast, but also the Sierra as caretakers of America's fledgling national parks before the birth of the National Park Service in 1916.

Funston Avenue Officers' Housing

The oldest, and some say the finest, grouping of Victorian houses in San Francisco stand along Funston Avenue. Built in 1862, these elegant, wooden-frame homes have housed the Army's officers for over a century.

San Francisco National Cemetery

Over 24,000 men lie buried in the green glades of the San Francisco National Cemetery. Among names inscribed on the smooth, white headstones is Congressman Phillip Burton, father of the GGNRA.

Lobos Creek

Lobos Creek brings rippling water, tadpoles, watercress, dragonflies, and other riparian wonders to the Presidio. This tranquil creek is the last free-flowing stream in San Francisco.

Enlisted men's barracks

Lobos Creek

Walks

The Presidio's many trails and roads (see map) offer visitors a variety of walking and cycling experiences, from forays deep into romantic forest glades to strolls along historic streetfronts.

Lover's Lane

Access: Begin in Pacific Heights at the intersection of Presidio and Pacific Avenues. Take Lover's Lane — the oldest trail in the Presidio — straight downhill to Barnard Avenue.

One Way: 1 mile/easy

Ecology Loop

Access: Begin at the Army Museum and walk up Funston Avenue along the Parade Ground. Continue up to Inspiration Point and El Polin Spring, and return via Lover's Lane.

Round trip: 2 miles/ easy

Presidio Historic Loop

For a complete tour of Presidio buildings and historic features, follow the route marked on the *Historic Trail Guide* available from the Army Museum.

Other Trails

From the bridge toll plaza area, hikers can drop down to the Golden Gate Promenade along the bayshore or pickup the Coastal Trail along the San Francisco Headlands.

Pointers

◆ In 1989, the Department of Defense announced the phased closure of the Presidio as an active military post. In accordance with existing law, the Presidio will gradually pass to the National Park Service as an invaluable addition to the geographical heart of the GGNRA.

Information:
Presidio Army Museum: 561-4115
Fort Point: 556-1693

GGNRA's Military History

In one afternoon trip to the GGNRA, visitors can walk through over 200 years of military history. The Bay Area has been a national defense priority second only to New York harbor for over a century. Between the Civil War and the Cold War, the military built forts, earthworks, look-out stations, and a host of other structures designed to protect California's resources and San Francisco's superb harbor from the enemy. GGNRA now encompasses the most complete and best preserved set of harbor defense installations in the United States.

Eras of Fortification

1790s –
Gold Rush

When the Spanish discovered the Bay in 1769, they declared San Francisco's harbor the best in the world. To protect this important resource, the Spanish built an adobe fort at Fort Point and earthworks at Fort Mason. The Mexican military took over the Spanish fortifications in 1822 when California became part of Mexico.

Weapons: Bronze cannon/range 0.5-1 mile
Best Examples: No fortifications in existence.

Gold Rush –
1860

With thousands of miles of wilderness between San Francisco and the rest of the nation (not to mention the embarrassment of the War of 1812), America invested a lot of money in the construction of the Bay Area's first harbor fortifications — two fortresses of brick and granite.

Weapons: Cannon/range 1-2 miles
Best Examples: Fort Point, Alcatraz

Civil War –
1870s

San Francisco's fear of a Confederate or British attack during the Civil War lead to the construction of earthen fortifications with underground powder magazines. These earth-

Black Point - Civil war Dress up

works were less vulnerable to modern rifled gunfire than the Bay's two brick forts.

Weapons: Cannon/range 2-3 miles
Best Examples: Battery Cavallo (East Fort Baker), Black Point Battery (Fort Mason)

1890s

Toward the end of the century, San Francisco began a massive program to upgrade the Golden Gate's defenses and built huge concrete emplacements for modern steel guns. This period of fortification was often called the Endicott era.

12" Disappearing Carriage Rifle

Weapons: Rifled mortars, barbette, and disappearing guns/range 8-10 miles
Best Examples: Batteries Mendell, Smith-Guthrie, Alexander (Marin Headlands), Battery Chamberlin (Baker Beach), Battery Godfrey (Fort Scott)

1930s –
World War II

With World War I came the threat of aerial attack, so artificial hills with dozens of feet of earth and concrete protection overhead were built to shield immense, long-range rifles.

16" Gun-Battery Davis

Weapons: 16-inch guns (2,100 pound shells)/range 27 miles
Best Examples: Battery Davis (Fort Funston), Battery Townsley (Fort Cronkhite)

Cold War –
1970

The Cold War and technological advances led to the installation of batteries for surface-to-air missiles guided by computers and radar.

Weapons: NIKE Ajax/range 75 miles, altitude 50,000 feet. NIKE Hercules/range 150 miles, altitude 200,000 feet
Best Examples: Site 88L (Marin Headlands)

Cannon - 1860's Fort Point

Glossary of Fortification Terms

Bunker: An underground fortification

Barbette Gun: Gun mounted so that it fires over a low wall, but remains exposed from the front and above

Battery: Grouping of guns or missiles

Casemate: Masonry structure which encloses a gun, leaving only a small opening for the gun to fire through

Disappearing Gun: Gun mounted so that when fired, the recoil action makes the carriage fold downward and disappear from view

Earthworks: Fortifications made primarily of sand and earth, with underground wood or masonry magazines

Fort: Army reserve (not just a building)

Gun: A weapon which fired a projectile in a straight line. Gun size descriptions in inches (e.g., 16-inch gun) are derived from measuring the diameter of their projectile

Magazine: Ammunition storage room

Mortar: Weapon which fires a projectile in a high arc

Parapet: Vertical wall in front of a gun

Projectile: Object fired from a gun or mortar

Rifling: Spiral groove etched inside the barrel of a gun that causes a projectile to spin when the gun is fired, giving it greater range and accuracy

GGNRA and the Military

Many of GGNRA's lands were once military reservations. Two Park properties — Fort Baker and Fort Mason — include small areas still actively used by the military. As these areas lie within the Park's legislated boundaries, any property within them which the Army no longer needs will pass directly to the GGNRA. The National Park Service is also preparing to receive a third major property from the Army — the Presidio. Transfer of the Presidio could begin as soon as 1991.

Periscope or Cormorant?

As army lore has it, a lone World War II soldier staring into the black night once spotted a tall, thin, black shape on the water. Convinced it was a submarine periscope, he fired.
Much disturbed, the "periscope" flew away.
Thus, for all San Francisco's military might, its only shot ever fired in anger during Word War II was aimed at a cormorant.

Golden Gate Bridge

Bridge Statistics	
Length of suspended portion	6,450 feet (1.22 miles)
Width	90 feet
Height of towers above water	746 feet
Number of strands in each cable	27,572
Total length of cable wire	80,000 miles
Sway	27.7 feet

The Golden Gate — the fabled harbor entrance to San Francisco Bay from the Pacific Ocean — was named almost a century before its more well-known namesake, the Golden Gate Bridge. One bright day in 1846, the beauty of this strait reminded General John Charles Fremont of Byzantium myths. The myths describe the great harbor entrance to Constantinople called the Golden Horn.

John Charles Fremont

Inspired by the visionary resemblance between these two port entrances, Fremont named the channel into San Francisco Bay the Golden Gate.

Few ships passed through the Golden Gate until the Gold Rush, when the sleepy little Pacific outpost of San Francisco became a boomtown overnight. More than a thousand vessels entered the Golden Gate between 1849 and 1850. As San Francisco grew and technology advanced, many dreamed of spanning the Golden Gate with a bridge.

But it took the vision and energy of engineer Joseph Strauss to make the dream come true. The first steam shovels set to work on the Marin anchorage in 1933. Completed four years later, construction of the bridge cost $35 million and the lives of eleven men. When the 1.2-mile-long suspension span opened to traffic on May 28, 1937, the Golden Gate Bridge took its place among the technological and engineering marvels of the world.

Joseph Strauss

Best Golden Gate Views

- Conzelman Road: A scenic drive along the Marin Headlands (see p. 56).

- Hawk Hill (Hill 129): Park and walk a short distance for top-of-the-world views from a coastal highpoint in the Marin Headlands (see p. 56).

- Point Bonita: Park and walk to the lighthouse for views of the golden gateway and edge of the continent (see p. 57).

- Bridge Vista Point: Park and look at San Francisco from the north side of the bridge.

- East Fort Baker: Park and walk around a tiny cove right under the Golden Gate (see p. 59).

- U.S.S. *San Francisco* Memorial Lot, Lands End: Park and view the Golden Gate from the west (see p. 40).

Construction of Golden Gate Bridge

San Francisco Headlands

GGNRA hugs the coastline west of Fort Point, encompassing rugged headlands, cypress forests, beaches, seacoast batteries, and the Cliff House.

S.F. Headlands serpentine outcrops

Serpentine

Outcrops of grey-green serpentine, an unusual rock type, protrude among the steep oceanfront cliffs between Fort Point and Baker Beach. Serpentine forms when certain minerals and rocks from deep in the earth's mantle come into contact with water as they are squeezed up toward the crust. On the earth's surface, serpentine yields soils unusually high in magnesium and low in calcium, producing many special adaptations and rare species among plants. The best views of San Francisco's serpentine cliffs are from the overlooks on Lincoln Blvd. north of Baker Beach.

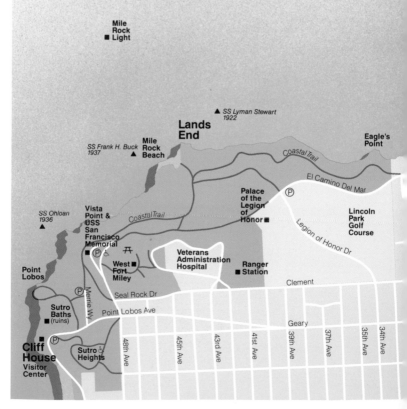

Mile Rock Light

SS Lyman Stewart 1922

Lands End

Eagle's Point

SS Frank H. Buck 1937

Mile Rock Beach

Coastal Trail

El Camino Del Mar

Palace of the Legion of Honor

Lincoln Park Golf Course

SS Ohloan 1936

Vista Point & USS San Francisco Memorial

Coastal Trail

Legion of Honor Dr

Point Lobos

Veterans Administration Hospital

West Fort Miley

Ranger Station

Clement

Seal Rock Dr

Point Lobos Ave

Merrie Wy.

Sutro Baths (ruins)

Geary

Cliff House
Visitor Center

Sutro Heights

48th Ave
45th Ave
43rd Ave
41st Ave
39th Ave
37th Ave
35th Ave
34th Ave

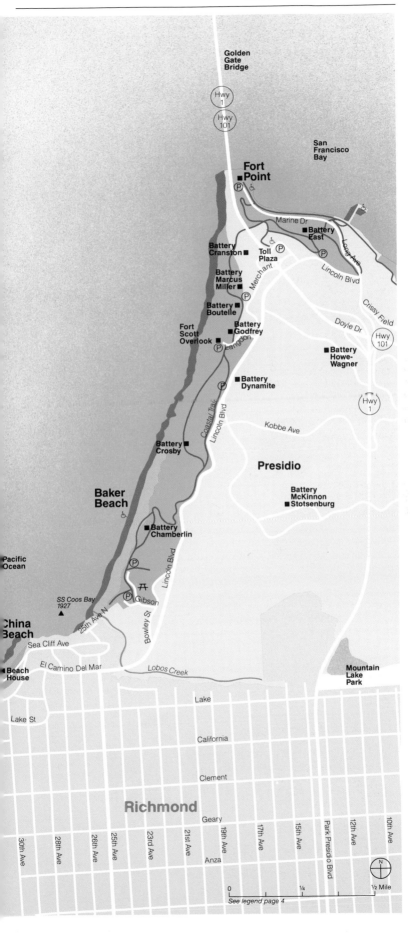

Golden
Gate
Bridge

Hwy
1

Hwy
101

San
Francisco
Bay

Fort
Point

Marine Dr

Battery
East

Battery
Cranston

Toll
Plaza

Lincoln Blvd

Battery
Marcus
Miller

Merchant

Crissy Field

Battery
Boutelle

Doyle Dr

Battery
Godfrey

Hwy
101

Fort
Scott
Overlook

Langdon

Battery
Howe-
Wagner

Battery
Dynamite

Coastal Trail

Lincoln Blvd

Hwy
1

Kobbe Ave

Battery
Crosby

Presidio

Baker
Beach

Battery
McKinnon
Stotsenburg

Pacific
Ocean

Battery
Chamberlin

Lincoln Blvd

SS Coos Bay
1927

Gibson

Bowley St

China
Beach

25th Ave N

Sea Cliff Ave

El Camino Del Mar

Lobos Creek

Mountain
Lake
Park

Beach
House

Lake

Lake St

California

Clement

Richmond

Geary

Anza

30th Ave
28th Ave
26th Ave
25th Ave
23rd Ave
21st Ave
19th Ave
17th Ave
15th Ave
Park Presidio Blvd
12th Ave
10th Ave

0   ¼   ½ Mile

N

See legend page 4

Baker Beach

Sunbathing
Walking
Picnicking
Surf fishing

Mile-long Baker Beach lies at the foot of the rugged serpentine cliffs just west of the Presidio. The view from the beach is spectacular, with the tawny wilds of the Marin Headlands and the Presidio flanking the sleek, orange span of the Golden Gate. Baker Beach visitors can also explore Battery Chamberlin's immense gun platforms.

The Beach

When the sun comes out, Baker Beach can be warm enough for sunbathing and picnicking. The strong riptides and sudden depths off-shore, however, make the water too dangerous for swimming. For fishermen, the surf often yields a fine catch.

Picnic Area

Tucked behind the cypress at the east end of the parking lot is a pleasant picnic area with tables and grills.

Battery Chamberlin

The army built Battery Chamberlin in 1903 to protect the harbor's minefields. The battery's "disappearing" guns could be cranked in and out of their camouflaged emplacement on the beach. In 1976, GGNRA received a 97,000-pound cannon which resembles Battery Chamberlin's early guns. When rangers open the battery, visitors can watch a demonstration of how this cannon's predecessors disappeared into the beachfront long ago. Occasionally, a ranger opens the small Chamberlin museum.

Battery Chamberlin, 1945

The only shark attack ever recorded in San Francisco took place at Baker Beach in 1959.

Pointers

◆ On weekends, be prepared for crowds and parking problems.

◆ During very low tides, it's possible to hike all the way to the Golden Gate Bridge on the beach.

◆ Hikers can pick up the Coastal Trail on the cliffside above Baker Beach.

The City's Water Supply

In the early days, many San Francisco residents got drinking water off out-of-town barges or from one of the 65 carriers who brought barreled water into town on mules. With the population boom of the Gold Rush, the city needed a larger and more dependable water supply. So a man named John Bensley dammed Lobos Creek at its mouth near Baker Beach and built a redwood flume to carry the water around to Black Point — completing the city's first permanent water supply in 1858.

Information:
556-8371

China Beach

Swimming
Sunbathing
Picnicking
Volleyball

C hina Beach is a tiny cove between Baker Beach and Lands End. It's the only safe place to swim in San Francisco, aside from Aquatic Park. The beach also offers good play spots for children and fine views of the Marin Headlands and the Golden Gate.

The Beach

China Beach's sheltered pocket of sand provides access to safe swimming waters and a place to stretch out or picnic in the sun. Lifeguards are on duty April through October. Public showers and changing rooms are also available.

Sun Deck

For those interested in sunbathing out of the wind, there's a small, protected deck at the China Beach lifeguard station.

Fog Formation

Fog forms when the warm, moist air brought by prevailing west winds encounters the chilly ocean waters off GGNRA's shores. Though fog occurs sporadically year-round, it mainly blankets San Francisco in the summer when hot inland temperatures create a low pressure zone over the Central Valley. The hot inland air rises, and the heavier cold ocean air rushes in to replace it. This flow from the high to the low pressure zone sucks the fog in through the Golden Gate and past China Beach.

Chinese Fishermen

Local residents named China Beach for the Chinese fishermen who anchored their junks in the cove and camped on the beach long ago. Rumor has it that the fishermen did more than catch fresh perch, bass, and flounder. Apparently, they also smuggled Chinese immigrants from ship to shore. Visitors can see a monument to these early cove-dwellers at China Beach.

Pointers

- China Beach appears on some maps as Phelan Beach; for a short period, the City renamed the beach to honor former Mayor and U.S. Senator James D. Phelan who fought to keep China Beach open to the public in the 1920s.

Information:
556-8371

Lands End

Walking
Picnicking
Birdwatching
Views
Shipwrecks

Lands End is the wildest, rockiest corner of San Francisco — a corner strewn with shipwrecks and rife with landslides. These coastal headlands west of the Golden Gate connect two popular landmarks: the Cliff House and the Palace of the Legion of Honor. At the tip of Lands End is Point Lobos, named by the Spanish for its many "lobos marinos" (sea wolves). The barks of these sea lions — as they're known today — still filter up from the rocks below. Trails at Lands End offer a clifftop walk through dark cypress and open grass with 30-mile views up and down the California coast.

Vista Point & U.S.S. *San Francisco* Memorial

The drive-in vista point just off El Camino Del Mar above the Cliff House presents grand views of the Pacific coast. At the wayside stands a memorial to the U.S.S. *San Francisco*. This heroic cruiser spearheaded a major sea battle during the Battle of Guadalcanal in 1942, sustaining 45 hits and 25 fires in combat. The names of the 107 men lost in the battle are engraved in the memorial, flanked by the actual shell-riddled bridge of the warship.

West Fort Miley Batteries and Picnic Area

West Fort Miley offers visitors a grassy picnic area among three turn-of-the-century gun emplacements. The area affords a splendid view of Ocean Beach. Visitors should park in the Vista Point parking lot, walk back a little along El Camino Del Mar, and take the first road to the left inland.

Beaches

A variety of shoreline pocket beaches lie at the foot of Lands End. Visitors can explore these sandy enclaves at low tide, but be careful not to get cut off by rising tides.

View from Lands End

Shipwreck Overlooks

Looking down at the rocky shoreline from the dizzy-ing heights of Lands End, visitors can see the remains of three shipwrecks. In the surf below stand Mile Rock and Point Lobos — the tips of two, vast, submerged, treacherous rocks. These rocks have pierced the hulls and sterns of many worthy vessels. When the freighter *Ohioan* cracked up at Point Lobos on a foggy night back in 1937, her steel hull hit the rocks so hard that sparks illuminated the night. In the 1920s and 1930s, first, the *Lyman Stewart*, and later, the *Frank Buck*, each ended their days on the exact same rock off

Wreck of the Ohioan, 1937

Lands End. Ironically, these two tankers also began their days together, side by side in the same shipyard. To see the *Ohioan's* rudder post and boilers, take the stairs up from the Sutro Baths platform to Point Lobos. To see the *Lyman Stewart's* triple expansion steam engine and the *Frank Buck's* rudder post and steam engine, keep an eye out from the Coastal Trail between the Vista Point and the Palace of the Legion of Honor.

Trails

Visitors can choose from a variety of Lands End trails for hikes through cypress forests and along the headlands.

Railroad Bed Loop
Features: Coastal views and cypress forest
Access: Start at the Palace of the Legion of Honor parking lot. Head west on El Camino Del Mar. The paved road becomes a dirt trail that leads to the vista area and U.S.S. *San Francisco* memorial. From this point, take the stairway down to the lower trail (Coastal Trail) which circles back along the old right-of-way of the Ferries and Cliff House Railroad.
Round trip: 1.0 miles/easy

Coastal Trail
Features: Coastal views
Access: Start at the Palace of the Legion of Honor. Take the Coastal Trail south along Lands End and Ocean Beach to Fort Funston.
One way: 10 miles/moderate

Fog Drip

Fog is an important source of moisture for many plants and trees in GGNRA, including those growing on the clifftops at Lands End. A third of the total moisture available to local plants is produced by fog drip — a phe-nomenon in which fog droplets condense on the leaves of redwood, fir, and coastal scrub. Many California native plants are specifically adapted to make the most of fog drip. Trillium, for exam-ple, thrives on drops falling from the red-wood forest overhead.

Pointers

♦ The cliffs at Lands End are highly un-stable. Footing is extremely treacher-ous, and many a climber has tumbled to his or her death off Lands End. Please be careful.

Ferries and Cliff House Railroad

Long ago, San Franciscans had to travel quite a distance on horseback or by carriage to spend a day at the seaside. Eventually, however, the building of the Ferries and Cliff House Railroad in the 1880s brought the seaside within easy reach of the local populace. For a nickel, peo-ple could climb into one of the railroad's open-air carriages and enjoy a clifftop ride around Lands End to the Cliff House or Ocean Beach.

Information:
556-8371

Cliff House

Ocean views
Walking
Dining
Sea lions
Seabirds
Visitor information

S ightseers from near and far flock to the Cliff House, a complex of oceanfront restaurants and shops between Lands End and Ocean Beach. San Franciscans have sipped champagne and admired ocean views from three successive Cliff Houses since 1863 — the first, an exclusive casino, the second, a Victorian palace built by millionaire Adolph Sutro in the 19th century. Though a third Cliff House replaced the palace long ago, visitors can still sample the grandeur of Sutro's waterfront empire by exploring the nearby gardens of Sutro Heights and the ruins of Sutro Baths.

The Cliff House

The Cliff House's giant glass windows present visitors with a direct view over the Pacific horizon, the perfect place, as one historian put it, "to confront nature from the comfort of an armchair." Apart from restaurants and bars, the Cliff House includes several gift shops.

The Visitor Center

Exhibits in the GGNRA visitor center on the oceanfront deck below the Cliff House tell the historical story of Sutro's unique empire. Additional exhibits feature shipwrecks, wildlife, and other subjects. The center also offers informational materials such as park guides, maps, and posters.

Seal Rocks

From the Cliff House and vista area, visitors can see and hear the sea lions on Seal Rocks. These slippery rocks bear a misleading name, as the sleek beasts sunning themselves below are not seals, but sea lions (see p. 44).

> *"The baths rival in magnitude, utility, and beauty the famous abluvian resorts of Titus, Caracella, or Diocletian. Thus has the tide been harnessed and made subservient to the multitudes."*
> An Admirer

Sutro Baths in their heyday, ca. 1897 (see opposite)

A Walking Tour of the Cliff House Area

Features: Sutro Heights, Sutro Baths, Cliff House, Ocean Beach

Access: Park at Merrie Way. Walk across Point Lobos Avenue and up the path to **Sutro Heights**. After strolling through the gardens, be sure to take the steps up to the parapet for a splendid view of Sutro's empire and Ocean Beach. Return to the avenue and continue down the oceanfront sidewalk to the ruins of **Sutro Baths**. Take the walkway through the ruins to Point Lobos and look for signs of shipwrecks. Return to Point Lobos Avenue. Walk to the Cliff House and down the stairway to the **Visitor Center** for a look at the exhibits and **Seal Rocks**. Continue south on the sidewalk in front of the Cliff House down to **Ocean Beach**. After a stroll along the Pacific surf, return to the **Cliff House** for refreshments.

Cliff House Walks with Rangers

Park rangers lead special walks for visitors interested in the natural and cultural history of the Cliff House area. Check for current schedule.

The Dune Tansy

Between June and September, the golden-yellow, button-shaped flowers of the dune tansy brighten the cliffs around Sutro Baths. Even prettier than the blossoms are the tansy's delicate, feathery leaves, thick with soft, silvery hairs. Years ago, people made tansy tea to cure colds, expel worms, treat hysteria, strengthen kidneys, and remedy other ailments.

Sutro Heights Garden

Though long years of neglect have taken a heavy toll, the quiet lawns and regal trees of Sutro Heights remain a pleasant picnic and rest stop, particularly for hikers and bicyclists on the Coastal Trail. The entrance to the garden is at 48th Avenue and Point Lobos. From the garden's parapet, visitors can enjoy unparalleled views down Ocean Beach and up the Marin coast. Though Adolph Sutro created the garden for his own pleasure in the 1880s, he invited the public to walk as they pleased among the exotic tree species, stone satyrs, and delicate flower beds of Sutro Heights. In Sutro's day, 17 gardeners maintained this enclave of greenery and stone. The garden still charms visitors with subtle traces of its former grandeur.

Sutro Baths Ruins

From the Cliff House walkways and overlooks, visitors can see the ruins of Sutro Baths — a lavish 25,000-person swimming facility built in the 19th century by Adolph Sutro. The facility's six, salt-water swimming tanks (ingeniously flushed by the tides), 517 private dressing rooms, restaurants, and arcades were enclosed by 100,000 square feet of glass. Patrons could rent one of 20,000 bathing suits to soak in a pool surrounded by rare tropical plants and foreign antiquities. Though destroyed by fire in 1966, the foundations of Sutro Baths are still visible on the rocks north of the Cliff House. Trails lead down to the ruins from the Merrie Way parking area.

Seabirds

From the Cliff House overlooks, visitors will see a wide variety of seabirds wheeling in the sky, skimming the wavecrests, and sitting on Seal Rocks offshore. Among these are thin, black cormorants, large, white gulls, and sometimes even brown pelicans. Seabirds depend on the ocean for food, fishing for nourishment among the waves and wetlands on GGNRA's coast.

Adolph Sutro — Mayor, Millionaire, Philanthropist

❏ Made fortune by designing tunnel that drained and ventilated silver mines in Nevada's Comstock Lode.

❏ Owned 1/12th of land in City and County of San Francisco.

❏ Built Cliff House, Sutro Baths, Sutro Heights Gardens, and Ferries and Cliff House Railroad.

❏ Served as San Francisco Mayor, 1894-1897. "He passed his term in a state of exasperation," wrote the *San Francisco Examiner.*

❏ Planted more than 250,000 trees as leading viticulturist and authority on arbor culture.

❏ Reputed to have owned the finest private library (250,000 volumes) in America.

Sea Lions

The California and Steller sea lions visible on Seal Rocks are just two of the many marine mammal species that live off GGNRA's coast. Comparing the two species, visitors will find Stellers lighter in color (particularly when wet) and more massive in the head, flippers, and body. The characteristics listed below are for adult males only. Females of both species, in a tradition characteristic of many mammals, are thinner in the shoulders and wider in the rear quarter.

California Sea Lions

Color Dry:	Light or dark brown
Color Wet:	Dark brown
Weight:	600-800 pounds
Length:	7-8 feet
Characteristics:	Prominent crest on scull
Occurrence:	Fall and Winter (visible all year)
Major Breeding Grounds in E. Pacific Ocean:	Channel Islands, Southern California down to Mazatlan and Tres Marias Island, Mexico

California

Steller Sea Lions

Color Dry:	Light tan or yellowish brown
Color Wet:	Light brown
Weight:	1,500-2,000 pounds
Length:	8-10 feet
Characteristics:	Large size; lighter coloration
Occurrence:	Late spring, summer, early fall
Major Breeding Grounds in E. Pacific Ocean:	Pribolof and Aleutian Islands, Alaska down to British Columbia, and South and Central California

Steller

The Three Cliff Houses

"The Cliff House....where but a single piece of glass seemed to separate the comforts and refinements of civilization and peace from the rude jarring of elemental discord and Nature in her rudest aspect, beyond."

Bret Harte, author

The second Cliff House - a Victorian Palace destroyed by fire in 1907.

The first Cliff House - A Scandalous Casino

A Scandalous Casino

The Cliff House of the 1860s and 1870s was an exclusive resort with fancy parlors and gambling casinos. At first, only San Francisco's most elite families patronized the resort, including, as author Karen Liberatore wrote, "the Crockers (of the bank), the Hearsts (of the paper), and the Stanfords (of the railroad), who could often be seen dining on terrapin stew or mussels Bordelaise." Later years brought a clientele more interested in gambling and the debauchery upstairs.

A Victorian Palace

The original Cliff House burned down in 1894 not long after Adolph Sutro bought the resort. Sutro built a Victorian palace in its place, an eight-story mansion crowned with fairy-tale turrets and towers. The new Cliff House had 20 private lunch rooms, numerous art galleries, several shops, even an elevator. Many a famous guest visited Sutro's clifftop chateau, including Oscar Wilde, Andrew Carnegie, and two American presidents.

A Modern Seaside Restaurant

The Cliff House fell into disrepair after Sutro died. Though the resort survived the 1906 earthquake with only $300 worth of damage, it burned to the ground a year later. Sutro's daughter built a neo-classical, concrete Cliff House among the ashes. In 1977, GGNRA acquired this third Cliff House. Today, the Cliff House continues to entertain patrons with dinner and sunset over the Pacific, while adjacent shops sell souvenirs of past and present.

Pointers

- Bring binoculars for close up views of the sea lions.
- Beware of slippery rocks and dangerous waves on the cliffs.
- Parking can be difficult by noon on summer weekends.

The Cliff House today

Information:
556-8642

The City's Pacific Shore

GGNRA's Pacific shore extends from the Cliff House to Fort Funston, Thornton Beach and beyond — a coastline of rough dunes, blustery beaches, and ocean frontage. Beyond Fort Funston, GGNRA reaches into the backbone of the Coast Range with the scenic hilltops of Sweeney and Milagra Ridges.

The "Other" Golden Gate Park

Golden Gate Park forms a long rectangle between San Francisco's Sunset and Richmond Districts. It's a city park, often confused with its neighboring national park — the GGNRA. Some of Golden Gate Park's features include lawns, woods, lakes, rose gardens, bike paths, tulip beds, tennis courts, exercise courses, windmills, boat rentals, an arboretum, the De Young Museum, the Planetarium, and the California Academy of Sciences (666-7200).

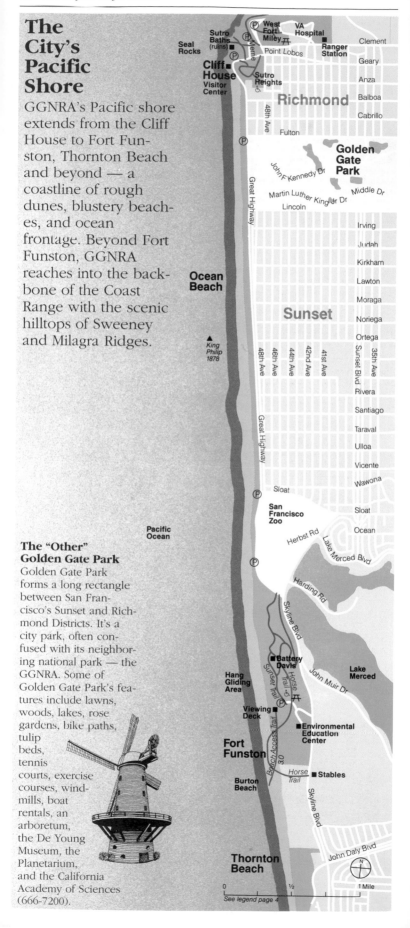

See legend page 4

Ocean Beach

Walking
Surfing
Sunbathing
Fishing
Volleyball
Jogging

Ocean Beach is the widest and longest expanse of sand on San Francisco's shores, extending from the Cliff House to Fort Funston along the Pacific Ocean. At one time, a vast sand dune wilderness (now the Sunset District) separated Ocean Beach from the rest of San Francisco. Today, Ocean Beach is popular for seaside drives, brisk jogs, and sunset walks.

The Beach

Ocean Beach visitors can not only sit or stroll by the water, but also fly kites and fish the surf. Occasionally, it's warm enough to lay in the sun. Most of the year, however, the beach's three miles of shoreline take the brunt of chilly west winds.

Dune grass and wildflowers on Ocean Beach

A Walk Along the Esplanade

An impressive esplanade tops the sea-wall along Ocean Beach, a remnant of the early days when the beach and Cliff House were part of a fashionable resort on the outskirts of town. The esplanade is a nice place for a walk along the water.

Shipwrecks on the Beach

Down at the foot of Ortega Street, visitors can see the worn ribs of the hull of the ship *King Philip* sticking out of the sand. Between 1850 and 1926, 20 different ships came to grief on Ocean Beach. It wasn't only the heavy surf that broke these shipwrecks into a thousand pieces. In those days, scavenging souvenirs from wrecks was one of San Francisco's most popular pastimes. In 1887, when the *Parallel* exploded near the Cliff House, 50,000 people turned out on Ocean Beach to pick her over.

Shipwreck *Aberdeen*, 1916

"...not a vestige of the wreck remained. Not so much as a floating barrel, bit of spar, or splinter of rail lay along the beach. Every bit of flotsam and jetsam had been carried off by the relic hunters..."
Parallel Crew Member

Pointers

♦ Swimming is not recommended at Ocean Beach due to dangerous rip tides.

♦ Attractions such as the Cliff House, Fort Funston, Golden Gate Park, and the city zoo all lie within walking distance of Ocean Beach.

♦ The best time of year for a walk on Ocean Beach is during Indian summer in September and October.

♦ Please be careful not to trample the fragile plants on the dunes. The National Park Service is trying to restore dune vegetation.

Information:
556-8371

Fort Funston

Walking
Picnicking
Horseback riding
Hang-gliding

Fort Funston is a rugged stretch of coastal headlands, sand, and dunes south of Ocean Beach. In some places, the dunes reach heights of 40 feet or more. These great, sandy bluffs, combined with the steady ocean breeze, make Fort Funston one of the premier hang-gliding spots in the nation. Hang-gliders fill the skies over Fort Funston's long beach, coastal trails, and sand-covered gun battery from March through October.

The Beach

At the foot of Fort Funston's cliffs is a wild and windy beach suitable for walking or horseback riding. Trails down to the beach scale the steep dunes with Dutch sand ladders (which help prevent erosion). Once on the beach, visitors can see shells, sand dollars, seaweed, and other signs of marine life.

Battery Davis

With the invention of aircraft, early open-air gun batteries became giant bull's-eye targets from the sky. So the army began building casemates over batteries to protect and camouflage them from enemy aircraft. Completed in 1938, Battery Davis was the first of these casemated batteries. The barrels of its two, massive, 16-inch guns weighed 146 tons apiece. Battery Davis served as the prototype for all 16-inch gun emplacements built in America after 1938. Fort Funston visitors can explore Battery Davis from the Sunset Trail.

The Viewing Deck

A spectacular wooden viewing deck hugs the hillside at Fort Funston. Right off the parking area, this deck offers views of soaring hang-gliders and the GGNRA coastline. The deck sits among base-end stations — used in military times to calculate the range of approaching ships.

Low Tide Loop Hike

Features: Coastal views, Battery Davis, beach, wildflowers
Access: At low tide, take the Sunset Trail north toward Ocean Beach. After passing through Battery Davis, continue north until the pavement ends. Follow the dune ridge down to the beach.

The Sunset Trail ♿

Fort Funston's paved Sunset Trail meanders along the ocean, the first wheelchair accessible trail to be built along the California coastline. This 0.75-mile-long, flat, seaside trail is easy for all members of the family. The trail takes visitors through Battery Davis, offering picnic tables and benches along the way.

Beach at Fort Funston

Walk south on the beach to below the hang-gliding area. Then, take the sand ladders back up to the parking lot.
Round trip: 2.5 miles/moderate

Spring Wildflower Walk

Springtime wildflowers of every color bloom at Fort Funston including poppies, lupine, Indian paintbrush, mock heather, sand verbena, seaside daisies, strawberries, and others.

Seaside Daisies

Sand Verbena

Beach Strawberry

Blue Bush Lupine

History of The Fort

When the first flag went up over the parade ground in the early 1900s, the *San Francisco Chronicle* remarked that Fort Funston looked more like a frontier post than anything else. Later, this unassuming place became a base for some heavy weaponry; first, the 16-inch guns of Battery Davis, and later, NIKE missiles. Today, the barracks have more benign occupants — the school-children attending Fort Funston's environmental education center.

Ranger programs

Hang-Gliding

Fort Funston is one of the nation's best hang-gliding spots, particularly for ridge soaring along the spectacular coast of California. The soaring season runs from late March through October while the west winds blow strongly. Fort Funston is a Hang-III (intermediate) site with a launch area and handicapped-accessible viewing deck. For those interested in learning more about this daring sport, several hang-gliding shops in the Fort Funston area offer instruction, sales, and repairs (see pp. 70-71).

Pointers

◆ Be prepared for strong winds.
◆ Look for GGNRA's new visitor center at Fort Funston, slated for construction in the near future.

Information:
556-8371

Sweeney Ridge & GGNRA South

Hiking
Picnicking
Bicycling
Horseback riding
Birding

The view from Sweeney Ridge is not only panoramic but also historic, for it was from this high point that Spanish explorer Gaspar de Portola discovered San Francisco Bay more than 200 years ago. GGNRA's parklands extend south from San Francisco to Thornton Beach and the peninsula coastline, and to Sweeney and Milagra ridges in the heart of San Mateo County. From these two high ridges between the Pacific Ocean and the Bay, hikers get superb views of the South Bay, the Pacific Coast, and the region's mountain ranges.

Sweeney Ridge

Sweeney Ridge is a hilly hiking area of ridges and ravines between San Bruno and Pacifica, about a 25-minute drive from San Francisco. The ridge's 1,200-foot-high summit, covered with coastal scrub and grassland, slopes down to the Bay on one side and to the Pacific on the other. Wildlife includes hawks, deer, and a plethora of springtime wildflowers.

San Francisco Bay Discovery Site

At the Bay discovery site on Sweeney's crest, visitors will find a stone plaque honoring Portola's expedition (see opposite). A nearby granite monument depicts the views from this scenic high spot which include the Farallon Islands, Mt. Tamalpais, Point Reyes, the South Bay, Mt. Diablo, the Montara Mountains, and San Pedro Point.

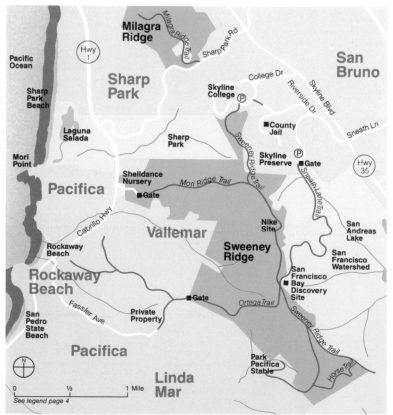

See legend page 4

Thornton Beach

Thornton Beach's sandy coastline and adjacent wind-protected valley make good turf for picnicking, beach walking, surf fishing, and flying remote-control gliders. The entrance to the beach is just south of Fort Funston. Visitors should park on Highway 35 (Skyline Boulevard) at the gate across from John Daly Boulevard and walk down.

Loop Hike to the Discovery Site

Access: Start at Student Lot #2 at Skyline College. Take the narrow paved road behind the lot up to the college's "Receiving" area and the trailhead. Follow the Sweeney Ridge Trail to the discovery site. Return via the paved Sneath Lane Trail. After the pedestrian gate, continue down Sneath Lane road. Take Riverside Drive left. Turn left at dead end, bear right at the fork around the county jail, and continue up to Skyline.
Round trip: 4 miles/moderate

Endangered Species

There are four endangered species in southern park areas — the Bay Checkerspot, Mission Blue, and San Bruno Elfin butterflies, and the San Francisco Garter Snake.

S.F. Garter Snake

Habitat:	Freshwater streams and marshes
Stomach:	Brilliant blue
Back:	Striped yellow and mossy green
Sides:	Continuous orange/brown stripes
Size:	2 feet long

Milagra Ridge

Milagra's open ridgeline slopes east-west, straight down to the Pacific coast. In the 1950s, Milagra's summit was flattened to accommodate a NIKE missile site controlled by radar on nearby Sweeney Ridge. This southern park area is open to pet-walkers and remote-control glider flyers. A mile-long, paved road leads to the ridgetop, offering easy access to all visitors, including the handicapped. The entrance to Milagra Ridge is at Sharp Park Road in Pacifica (at College Drive).

The Discovery of San Francisco Bay

In July 1769, Captain Gaspar de Portola headed north from Baja, California to set up missions in San Diego and Monterey Bay. When Portola reached Monterey Bay in October, he failed to recognize it and marched on northwards. A month later, while the expedition rested at San Pedro Creek, a scouting party reported sighting an "enormous arm of the sea." On November 4, Portola climbed Sweeney Ridge to see this great body of water for himself, and from that viewpoint, the New World's explorers got their first sight of San Francisco Bay.

Coyote Brush

Walks with Rangers

GGNRA rangers lead a number of monthly Sweeney Ridge walks with special themes such as wildflowers, birds, or history. Call for current schedule.

Pointers

◆ GGNRA's legislated boundary calls for gradual expansion of the Park into other areas of Daly City and San Mateo County. Check for current information regarding National Park Service management and public access to southern park areas.

Information:
556-8371

North of the Golden Gate

Tomales Bay

Marshall Petaluma Rd

See map page 88

Hwy

Inverness

Sir Francis Drake Blvd

Point Reyes Station

Point Reyes Rd

Novato Blvd

Hwy 37

Nicasio Valley Rd

Novato

Nicasio Reservoir

Point Reyes National Seashore

Olema

Lucas Valley Rd

Hwy 101

San Pablo Bay

Drakes Bay

Olema Valley

Sir Francis Drake Blvd

Kent Lake

Marin Municipal Water District

See map pages 72-73

San Rafael

Hwy

Audubon Canyon Ranch

Alpine Lake

See map pages 54-55

Pacific Ocean

Mt Tamalpais State Park

Bolinas Lagoon

Panoramic Hwy

Hwy 17

Bolinas

Stinson Beach

Muir Woods

Mill Valley

Rocky Point

Tennessee Valley

Tiburon

Muir Beach

Sausalito

Rodeo Beach

Marin Headlands

East Fort Baker

Angel Island

Golden Gate Bridge

N

0   2½   5 Miles

See legend page 4

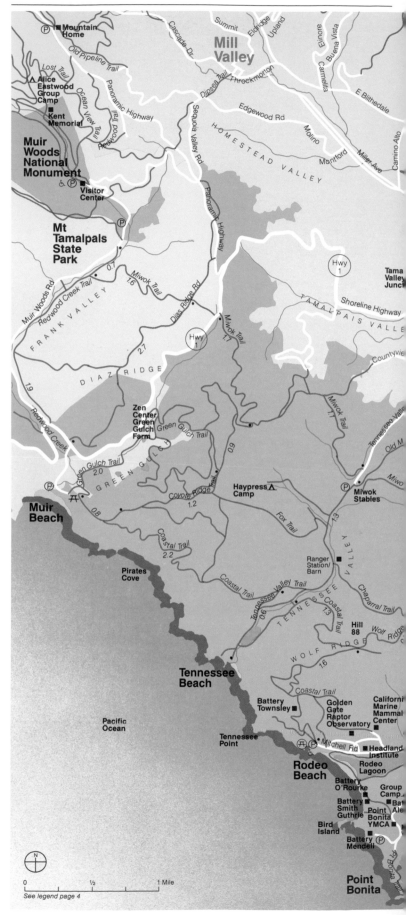

Mountain Home

P

Old Pipeline Trail

Lost Trail

Ocean View Trail

△ Alice Eastwood Group Camp

Kent Memorial

Cascade Dr

Summit

Eldridge

Upland

Mill Valley

Elinore

Buena Vista

Carmelita

E Blithedale

Panoramic Highway

Dipsea Trail

Throckmorton

Camino Alto

Edgewood Rd

Molino

HOMESTEAD VALLEY

Montford

Miller Ave

Muir Woods National Monument

♿ P

Visitor Center

Sequoia Valley Rd

Mt Tamalpals State Park

P

0.7

Miwok Trail 1.6

Muir Woods Rd

Redwood Creek Trail

FRANK VALLEY

Diaz Ridge Rd

Panoramic Highway

Hwy 1

Tama Valley Junct

TAMALPAIS VALLE

Shoreline Highway

Miwok Trail 1.7

Hwy 1

Countyvie

DIAZ RIDGE

2.7

1.9

Redwood Creek

Zen Center Green Gulch Farm

Green Gulch Trail

Green Gulch Trail

0.9

Miwok Trail 1.1

Tennessee Valle

Old M

Miwo

Green Gulch Trail 2.0

GREEN GULCH

Haypress △ Camp

Coyote Ridge 1.2

Fox Trail

P Miwok Stables

1.3

Muir Beach

P

⛩

0.8

Coastal Trail 2.2

Ranger Station/ Barn

VALLEY

Chaparral Trail

Pirates Cove

Coastal Trail

Tennessee Valley Trail

0.6

TENNESSEE Coastal Trail 1.3

WOLF RIDGE

Hill 88

Wolf Ridge

1.6

Tennessee Beach

Coastal Trail

Battery Townsley ■

Golden Gate Raptor Observatory

Californi Marine Mammal Center

Pacific Ocean

Tennessee Point

⛩ P

Mitchell Rd ■ Headland Institute

Rodeo Beach

Rodeo Lagoon

Battery O'Rourke ■

Group Camp ■

Battery Smith Guthrie ■

Point Bonita YMCA

■ Ba Ale

Bird Island

Battery Mendell ■ P

Point Bonita

⊕ N

0   ½   1 Mile

See legend page 4

Marin Headlands

GGNRA lands in southern Marin County encompass coastal headlands and bluffs, rural backcountry, windswept ridges, tiny coves, lagoons, beaches, seacoast fortifications, and spectacular vista points.

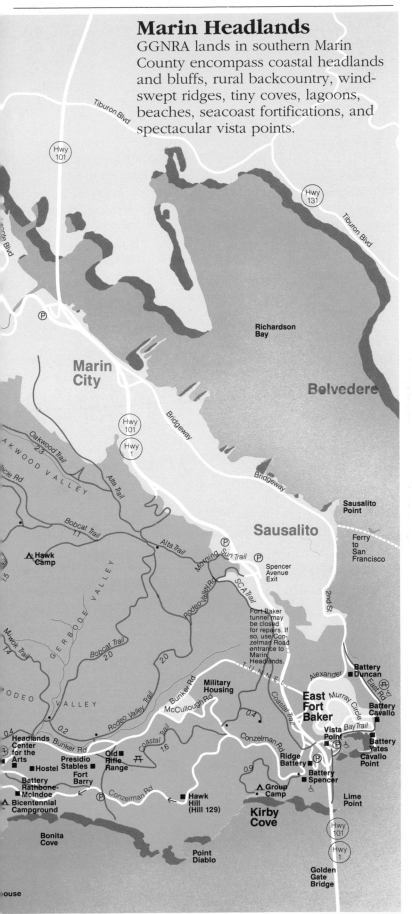

Tiburon Blvd

Hwy 101

Hwy 131

Tiburon Blvd

Richardson Bay

Marin City

Belvedere

Bonita Blvd

Hwy 101

Hwy 1

OAKWOOD VALLEY

Oakwood Trail 2.3

Alta Trail

cle Rd

Bridgeway

Bridgeway

Sausalito Point

Sausalito

Ferry to San Francisco

Bobcat Trail 1.1

Alta Trail

Hawk Camp

Morning Sun Trail

Alta Trail

P

P

Spencer Avenue Exit

SCA Trail

GERBODE VALLEY

Miwok Trail 1.4

Rodeo Valley Rd

Fort Baker tunnel may be closed for repairs. If so, use Conzelman Road entrance to Marin Headlands.

Bobcat Trail 2.0

2.0

Bunker Rd

Rodeo Valley Trail

T U N N E L

Alexander

2nd St

Battery Duncan

Military Housing

McCullough Rd

Coastal Trail

0.4

East Fort Baker

Murray Circle

East Rd

Battery Cavallo

RODEO VALLEY

0.4   0.2

Headlands Center for the Arts

Bunker Rd

Coastal Trail 1.6

Conzelman Rd

Vista Point

Bay Trail

Battery Yates

Cavallo Point

Hostel

Presidio Stables

Old Rifle Range

Ridge Battery

P

B

Battery Yates

Battery Rathbone-McIndoe

Fort Barry

P

Conzelman Rd

Hawk Hill (Hill 129)

0.9

Battery Spencer

Bicentennial Campground

Group Camp

Kirby Cove

Lime Point

Bonita Cove

Point Diablo

Hwy 101

Hwy 1

Golden Gate Bridge

ouse

Marin Headlands

Hiking
Picnicking
Beachcombing
Birdwatching
Vistas
Seacoast
  fortifications

J ust a few minutes drive beyond the Golden Gate, Marin County's southern headlands tower over the Pacific Ocean. No other neighbor of San Francisco affords such breathtaking views of the city in all its fairy-tale splendor. The Headlands have something for every-one: trails to hike, birds to watch, places to camp, roads to bike, beaches and seacoast fortifications to explore, and a thousand spots from which to survey GGNRA's scenic riches.

Scenic Conzelman Road and Hawk Hill

Visitors can drive cliff-hugging Conzelman Road from the Golden Gate to Point Bonita — all the way along the Bay's narrow entrance channel. This five-mile road climbs high above the bridge towers, offering an astounding bird's-eye view of San Francisco. Vista points along Conzelman include: Battery Spencer at the crest of the first hill; several road turn-outs; and Hawk Hill (Hill 129), 1.8 miles from the Golden Gate Bridge. At the spot where the road narrows to one lane and plunges headfirst down the coastline, visitors can park and walk up the concrete fire road to the top of Hawk Hill.

Kirby Cove

Kirby Cove nestles at the foot of the Marin Headlands just west of the Golden Gate. The mile-long trail to Kirby Cove descends 300 feet through a grove of cy-press, eucalyptus, and pine. At the cove, visi-tors will find a pristine wedge of beach, group camping facilities com-plete with tent pads, and a fabulous view of the Golden Gate Bridge from below.

Seacoast Fortifications Tour

Almost any walk in the Marin Headlands will bring visitors face-to-face with the overgrown structures and subterra-nean chambers of aban-doned military fortifica-tions. Rangers lead tours of a restored NIKE mis-sile site and other gun emplacements and sup-port facilities. For more details on the area's mil-itary history and a com-plete self-guided tour, see pp. 32-33 and 60-61.

Headlands Car-Free

Visitors can leave their cars behind and explore Rodeo Valley and the Marin Headlands backcountry on foot via the Coastal Trail. Leave the car (or get off the bus) at the small trailhead parking area on the west side of Highway 101 across from Vista Point. Follow signs up across Conzelman Road and into the Headlands.

Battery Wallace Picnic Area

This battery near the Point Bonita trailhead is one of the most scenic picnic spots in the entire GGNRA, offering visitors tables and grills overlooking the Golden Gate Bridge. (Site has no water.)

Coastal Trail

Point Bonita Lighthouse

The half-mile walk to Point Bonita Lighthouse takes visitors along a narrow ridge, through a hand-chiseled tunnel, and over a heart-stopping suspension footbridge to what seems like the end of the world. California's coastline stretches north and south, the Pacific rolls away to the west; and San Francisco glitters far inland. The lighthouse was first constructed in 1855 after San Francisco's infamous fog sent many a ship crashing against the rocky shores of Point Bonita. The first lighthouse keepers fired a cannon every half hour in foggy weather, day and night. This western sentinel now operates automatically, sending a revolving beam of bright light out into the fog and issuing periodic booms. Apart from the lighthouse, sights along the trail include an historic Coast Guard rescue station, wildflowers, and pillow basalt rock formations. Visitors can take a guided tour or explore the lighthouse on their own. Check times of tours and opening.

"I cannot find anyone here to relieve me, not five minutes; I have been up three days and nights, had only two hours rest. I'm nearly used up."
Ponit Bonita Fog Cannon Keeper, 1855

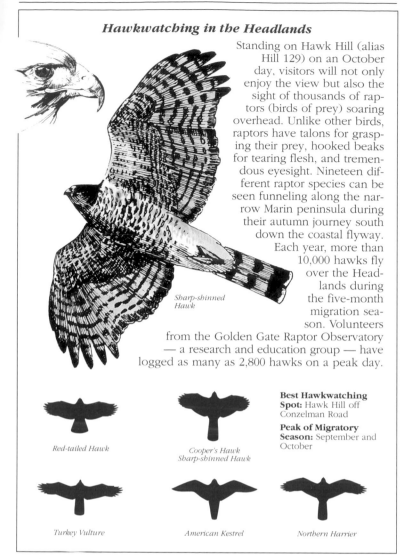

Hawkwatching in the Headlands

Standing on Hawk Hill (alias Hill 129) on an October day, visitors will not only enjoy the view but also the sight of thousands of raptors (birds of prey) soaring overhead. Unlike other birds, raptors have talons for grasping their prey, hooked beaks for tearing flesh, and tremendous eyesight. Nineteen different raptor species can be seen funneling along the narrow Marin peninsula during their autumn journey south down the coastal flyway. Each year, more than 10,000 hawks fly over the Headlands during the five-month migration season. Volunteers from the Golden Gate Raptor Observatory — a research and education group — have logged as many as 2,800 hawks on a peak day.

Sharp-shinned Hawk

Red-tailed Hawk

Cooper's Hawk
Sharp-shinned Hawk

Best Hawkwatching Spot: Hawk Hill off Conzelman Road

Peak of Migratory Season: September and October

Turkey Vulture

American Kestrel

Northern Harrier

Rocks from the Seafloor

The sea cliffs and road cuts of the Marin Headlands have some of the finest exposures of pillow basalt and chert to be found anywhere. Millions of years ago, these rocks formed around mid-ocean ridges several thousand miles from the West Coast at the bottom of the sea. The black pillow basalt formed when volcanic vents spewed lava onto the seafloor. Upon contact with the cold water, the lava solidified into pillow-shaped deposits of basalt. The red-brown radiolarian chert formed as layer upon sedimentary layer of skeletal remains from radiolarians (microscopic protozoans) collected on the seafloor. The seafloor moved slowly east (at about the rate a fingernail grows), sliding under the North American continent and leaving scrapings of radiolarian chert and pillow basalt behind.

Pillow Basalt Outcrops: Kirby Cove, Point Bonita

Chert Outcrops: Kirby Cove

Information:
Marin Headlands Visitor Center: 331-1540
Golden Gate Raptor Observatory: 331-0730

Pointers

♦ The far end of Conzelman Road closes every night around sunset and opens again at 7:30 am.

♦ For in-depth camping information, see pp. 68-69.

♦ Be prepared for weather fluctuating between sunshine and fog, particularly in the summer.

♦ Please reserve campgrounds well in advance (maximum 90 days).

♦ Beware of poison oak.

♦ Watch out for dangerous waves at the seashore.

♦ Cliffs are hazardous and unsuitable for climbing.

East Fort Baker

Ship watching
Fishing
Picnicking

E ast Fort Baker is an old army post in a picturesque bayshore cove under the Golden Gate Bridge. Apart from a popular fishing pier, East Fort Baker's public amenities include a number of grassy areas and coastal bluffs for picnicking. Nearby, the Lime Point Light and foghorn sit under the bridge in the flat spot once slated for Fort Point's counterpart in Marin.

Shoreline bluffs, East Fort Baker

Fog-Free Areas

East Fort Baker's best kept secret is that it's often sunny when western park areas are fogged in. Several other park areas often escape the fog: Bolinas Ridge, the Olema Valley, and the top of Mt. Tamalpais.

Golden Gate to Sausalito Trail

Features: Views, East Fort Baker
Access: Take the Coastal Trail from the Golden Gate Bridge Vista Point down to East Fort Baker. Follow the Bay Trail signs along Horseshoe Cove, behind Battery Cavallo and north to Sausalito Point.
One Way: 2 miles/ moderate

Fishing Pier

A fishing pier juts out from East Fort Baker's  shore, a good spot to catch perch, flounder, smelt, salmon, and rock crabs.

Seacoast Batteries

On the eastern bayshore, visitors will find the brick fortifications of Battery Cavallo and the concrete gun emplacements of Battery Yates (see pp. 60-61).

Pointers

◆ Please respect those areas of East Fort Baker that remain under Army jurisdiction, which include housing and the yacht club.
◆ In the next few years, the Bay Area Discovery Museum for children will be opening in East Fort Baker. Check for current information.

Picnic Spots

The grassy parade ground and coastal bluffs of East Fort Baker make quiet picnic spots out of the wind. Those who prefer picnic tables will find them near the Lime Point parking area and on East Road.

Ship and Sailboat Watching

East Fort Baker is a ship-watching grandstand beyond compare. West of the fort, Lime Point offers eye-level views of cargo ships, tankers, and luxury liners passing in and out under the Golden Gate. The bayshore bluffs to the east afford fine views of yachts and fancy sailboats, particularly on race days.

Information:
Marin Headlands Visitor Center: 331-1540

Marin Headlands Seacoast Fortifications Tour

Throughout much of local military history, the fortifications of the Marin Headlands were a necessary complement to the gun emplacements on San Francisco's shores. Military strategists felt that if enemy ships could be kept out of the strait of San Francisco, the city would remain safely beyond the range of hostile guns. As a result, the Marin Headlands came to host a wide variety of seacoast fortifications, ranging from 1870s earthwork batteries to NIKE missile launch sites.

To see a representative sample of these fortifications, visitors can take a half-day drive through the Headlands, stopping here and there to explore on foot. Bring a flashlight. If it's early or late in the day, or if the weather is foggy, check with Park rangers to make sure Conzelman Road is open. (See map pp. 54-55).

● Start by driving down to East Fort Baker on Bunker Road. Turn right at the parade ground and left on Murray Circle. Take the first right at the Bay Area Discovery Museum offices and continue up and around the marina to the concrete gun platforms of **Battery Yates** (1905-1946). Yates' six rapid-fire guns were sited so they could duel with enemy torpedo boats or destroyers

entering the Gate. Hidden in the bayfront hillside above are the parapets, magazines, meadows, and gun emplacements of **Battery Cavallo** (1872-1876). This post-Civil War earthwork fortification is only open for guided tours as it now serves as a vital habitat for the endangered Mission Blue Butterfly.

● Go back and drive along the parade ground. Surrounding this wide, flat lawn are the elegant homes

and administrative buildings of **Fort Baker**, most of which were

Fort Baker, ca.1924

constructed after 1895. The post provided everything needed by the men who fired the guns, including a church, hospital, bakery, gymnasium, and blacksmith shop.

● Take Bunker Road back uphill. Turn right on Alexander Avenue and continue through the Highway 101 underpass. Just before the bridge entrance, bear right up Conzelman Road. Park at the turnout on the first crest, where brick buildings mark the entrance to **Battery Spencer** (1897-1943). Walk through the concrete pillars and out past the 1870s brick

Battery Spencer

parapets of **Ridge Battery.** Farther along, visitors will find Spencer's gun platforms. The bolts which held the battery's three, 12-inch caliber guns in place still protrude from round, rusty mounts.

● Continue west on Conzelman Road. At the highest point on the ridge, just before the road becomes one way, lies **Battery Construction No. 129** (1942-1943), also known as **Hawk Hill.** Never completed, 129 was the last battery built in the Marin Headlands. Visitors can park and explore 129's massive

entrance tunnels and casemates, designed to protect the guns from aerial bombardment while retaining the natural appearance of the hillside. Be sure to walk up the adjacent dirt road to see the unparalled vistas from the top of 129.

● Continue driving down the one-way section of Conzelman Road past **Battery Rathbone-McIndoe** (1905-1948), whose four, 6-inch guns protected the minefields outside the Golden Gate during World War II.

● At the end of the dirt section of Conzelman, bear right and then left onto the pavement of Field Road. Follow the road past the YMCA Point Bonita Center and continue up to the concrete pillars and platforms of **Battery Mendell** (1905-1943). The battery was named for Colonel George Mendell who supervised construction of the post-Civil War and Endicott era batteries around the Bay. Mendell's colonnades, stairs, and concrete slabs offer a superb destination for military history enthusiasts. Beware of the sheer drop from the front of the gun pits to the Pacific surf!

● Return down Field Road and continue to the left. Stop at the first wayside exhibit on the left for a view of **Battery Bravo** (1954-1974) over the fence. Battery Bravo is one of two Cold War-era NIKE missile sites in the Headlands. From above, visitors can see the two, yellow-and-green launch rails, the elevator doors to the missile storage areas below ground, and the area between two fences once patrolled by attack dogs.

● Drive down to Bunker Road. Those who wish to continue ex-

Fort Barry - 1955

ploring can turn left and visit **Fort Cronkhite** (1937-1973) — the support community and barracks for Headlands fortifications, and **Battery Townsley** (1939-1948) — the first battery on the Pacific coast to fire a 16-inch projectile. Those who wish to return to Highway 101 can turn right.

View from Battery Townsley

Rodeo Valley

Beachcombing
Birdwatching
Hiking
Visitor information
Seabirds

Running east to west, Rodeo Valley is a long, low dip in the heart of the Marin Headlands. The valley opens into a lagoon and beach at the seashore. Two military forts once guarded Rodeo Valley's smooth hills and quiet shores. Fort Barry and Fort Cronkhite, whose structures now serve as park facilities, were nerve centers of Marin Headlands military activities long ago. Rodeo Valley is still a focal point of the Marin Headlands, a place where visitors can park and walk to the beach, the backcountry, a lighthouse, the visitor center, and coastal bluffs.

Marin Headlands Visitor Center

At the recently-opened visitor center in the Fort Barry Chapel visitors can get hiking and camping information, join special walks, examine the center's natural history exhibits, and buy posters, books, and other park-related items.

Rodeo Beach

Rodeo Beach is easily accessible to young and old. This pebbly, Pacific beach offers good picnic spots, wind for kite flying, and nearby bluffs for hikes and wave-watching. Beachcombers will see jasper, carnelian, black agate, and jade underfoot.

Picnic Areas

Rodeo Pond: On the east side of the car bridge across Rodeo Lagoon are some picnic tables and toilets.

Rodeo Beach: The picnic site just off the Rodeo Beach parking area overlooks the beach. The site's tables, grills, water, and toilets are all handicapped accessible.

Rifle Range: The old military rifle range in the heart of Rodeo Valley provides a pleasant, grassy picnic spot out of the wind. First-come, first-served. Large groups can reserve this day-use area, taking priority over individual picnickers.

Birdwatching Spots

Rodeo Lagoon and Bird Island are favorite bird-watching spots in the Rodeo Valley area. Just offshore, Bird Island's guano-white crags throng with cormorants, gulls, and brown pelicans. The clifftop trail overlooking the island is one of the best pelican-watching locations on the West Coast, with up to 1,200 of these great, brown birds settling on the rocks at one time. Inland, visitors can see egrets, ducks, and other birds feeding and resting in the shallow wetlands of Rodeo Lagoon.

Brown Pelican

Body Color:
Brown/grey

Head Color:
Grey/white

Bill: Long

Wingspan: 7 feet

Special Status:
USFGS-listed rare species

Occurrence:
Summer, early winter

Trails

Rodeo Beach is an excellent starting point for hikes over scenic ridge tops, across open grasslands, along the coastline, and away from the hustle and bustle of the big city next door.

Rodeo Lagoon Loop

Features: Birds, lagoon, coastal scrub, poison oak
Access: Start near the lagoon footbridge. Take the footbridge across to Rodeo Beach and walk along the lagoon edge. Bear left up the trail closest to the lagoon and continue all the way around.
Round trip: 1.5 miles/easy

Coastal Trail/ Hill 88 Loop

Features: Coastal views, Battery Townsley, wildflowers
Access: Start at the Rodeo Beach parking area. Take Coastal Trail north past Battery Townsley. Return via Wolf Ridge and Miwok Trails.
Round trip: 4.3 miles/ moderate

Walks with Rangers

Rangers lead a variety of special walks through the Marin Headlands every month with themes ranging from birding, wildflowers, and waterfalls to coastal batteries. Call for current schedule.

Rodeo Beach & Lagoon

Pointers

◆ Muni bus #76 provides transportation from the Transbay Terminal and Lombard Street in San Francisco to Rodeo Beach on Sundays and holidays.

◆ Be prepared for weather fluctuating between sunshine and fog, particularly in the summer.

◆ Watch out for ticks and poison oak.

◆ Many old fire and ranch roads in the Headlands are good for mountain biking. Please give way to hikers, horses, and walkers sharing the trail. Biking is prohibited on footpaths and open terrain. Check for current regulations.

◆ For more camping information, see pp. 68-69.

Park Partners

GGNRA shares the surplus army buildings in Rodeo Valley with a variety of nonprofit groups.

California Marine Mammal Center: Offers close-up views of sick and injured marine mammals, as well as visitor center with slide show and educational exhibits.

Golden Gate Hostel: Offers low cost accommodations for travelers of all ages.

Golden Gate Raptor Observatory: Conducts research and educational programs about the hawk migration.

Headlands Institute: Offers residential, environmental education programs at the seashore for school kids.

Headlands Center for the Arts: Provides opportunities for artists to explore the Marin Headlands and make their interpretations accessible to the public.

Pacific Energy and Resource Center: Displays energy-related exhibits and conducts conservation and alternative energy technology research.

YMCA Point Bonita Outdoor and Conference Center: Hosts conferences, retreats, environmental education programs, YMCA camps, and other group activities.

Information:
Marin Headlands Visitor Center: 331-1540
California Marine Mammal Center: 331-7325
Golden Gate Hostel: 331-2777
Golden Gate Raptor Observatory: 331-0730
Headlands Institute: 332-5771
Headlands Center for the Arts: 331-2787
Pacific Energy and Resource Center: 332-8200
YMCA Point Bonita Outdoor Center: 331-9622

Gerbode Valley and Backcountry

**Hiking
Vistas
Wildflowers
Camping**

Just inside the coastal zone of the Marin Headlands lies GGNRA's wilderness backcountry — a hiker's paradise. An extensive network of trails traverse this landscape of grassland and coastal chaparral. Every hilltop is a panoramic vista point; every valley is a chance to smell fennel and sage, or catch a fleeting glimpse of a bobcat or bush rabbit.

The Gerbode Valley

At the heart of the backcountry lies one of the prettiest valleys in the area — the Gerbode. GGNRA recently began planting native bunch grass on the valley floor — an area overrun by the tougher, hoof-proof, grazing grasses introduced by the Spanish long ago. The planting project is part of a park-wide effort to replace exotic plant species introduced from other areas with species native to the region.

Black-tail Deer

Black-tail deer, a subspecies of mule deer, range throughout GGNRA's Marin areas. These large-eared, black-tailed, brown-bodied deer stand 3-3.5 feet tall and weigh 100-200 pounds. Dusk is the best time for visitors to see the deer roaming GGNRA's open grasslands.

Bobcats

Though bobcats are largely creatures of the night, they can often be seen on the Marin peninsula during the day, streaking across the chaparral or basking in the sun. These furry predators hunt rodents, rabbit, and other small mammals. Bobcat paw marks and scat dot the Headlands, but many visitors mistake their tracks for those of the more elusive mountain lion — a feline with larger paws and a longer tail. Bobcats are most likely to be seen in the Gerbode and Tennessee Valley areas on nice spring and summer days.

Trails

Backcountry hikes offer views of varied terrain and a chance to see hawks, bobcats, and other animals in the wilder corners of the park. The main trailhead for Gerbode Valley hikes is Rodeo Valley. See Tennessee Valley and Rodeo Valley sections for alternate hikes.

Indian Paint-brush

Miwok Loop

Features: Wildlife, backcountry scenery, wildflowers

Access: Start in Rodeo Valley on the north side of the car bridge between the pond and lagoon on Bunker Road. Take the Miwok Trail up over the ridge, past the white VORTAC (aircraft guidance) building. Return via the Bobcat Trail.

Round trip: 6.8 miles/moderate

Morning Sun Loop

Features: Wildlife, backcountry scenery, wildflowers

Access: Start at the Spencer Avenue Exit off Highway 101 (see Pointers below). Take the Morning Sun and Rodeo Valley Trails to Fort Barry. Return via the Miwok and Bobcat Trails.

Round trip: 4.5 miles/moderate

Wildflowers

In the spring, GGNRA bursts out in bright colors, particularly in the Marin Headlands. Two floral provinces overlap in the park, dramatically increasing the number of wildflower species. GGNRA's foggy coasts and dry interiors, its hodge-podge of soils, and its many fresh and salt-water zones provide an unusual diversity of wildflower and rare plant habitats. Some of the best wildflower walks are on the Point Bonita Lighthouse, Tennessee Valley, Coastal, Wolf Ridge, and Miwok Trails.

California Buttercup / yellow

Star Zigadene / white

Milkmaids / white

Blue-eyed Grass / deep purple

Ground Iris / purple

Sun Cup / yellow

Red Maids / red

Pointers

- Beware of poison oak, ticks, and an occasional rattlesnake.
- Golden Gate Transit buses #20 and #80 stop at the trailhead at Spencer Avenue off Highway 101.
- Take water on hiking trips.
- Be prepared for weather fluctuating between sunshine and fog, particularly in the summer.

California Poppy

Information:
Marin Headlands Visitor Center: 331-1540

Tennessee Valley

Walking
Bicycling
Picnicking
Horseback riding
Hiking

T ennessee Valley meanders for two miles through serene, rolling hills down to a tiny cove. Out under the surf, off the cove's black beach, lies the shipwreck of the S.S. *Tennessee*, the namesake of this valley. The valley's wide, well-groomed trail offers an easy walk, bike, or horseback ride to the ocean.

Red Willow

Eucalyptus

The Valley

A creek bordered with eucalyptus and willow flows through Tennessee Valley. Visitors can walk along this pretty, tree-lined waterway for a short distance on a side path.

The Lagoon

The path forking left near the end of the main trail leads over an earthen dam and around a stock pond and lagoon. Mallard ducks, coots, sea gulls, and other birds frequent these sheltered, wetland waters.

The Cove

Sandwiched between the bluffs on either side of Tennessee Cove lies a pocket beach. The view from the cove encompasses wave-lashed rocks and the jagged edge of Marin County.

The Shipwreck

It was a grey Sunday morning in March 1853 when the fog lifted just enough to show Captain Mellus of the S.S. *Tennessee* that he'd missed the Golden Gate and was about to collide with an unknown shore. Rather than crash against the rocks, the captain steamed his vessel right up onto the beach at what is now Tennessee Cove. All 550 passengers climbed safely off the ship onto dry land. There was even time to salvage 14 chests of gold before heavy surf broke *Tennessee's* oak hull to pieces. Occasionally, the shifting sands expose the ship's massive cast-iron engine at the southern end of the cove.

...there came an awful crash of the steamer. Everybody knew instantly we'd struck. Everything went off the table in a heap, and this nurse, she went over too, baby and all....then she made a jump for my chum and flung her arms around his neck, and yelled "O, Save me, save me! I'm going to be drowned!" "O, no" says he, "you won't drown. You're too fat, you'll float."

Fred Stocking, Passenger, S.S. *Tennessee*

Tennessee Valley Beach

Trails

The Tennessee Valley trail connects with several scenic loop hikes over coastal terrain. The valley is an excellent starting point for hikes to Muir Beach, Rodeo Beach, and the Gerbode backcountry (see map pp. 54-55).

> Look for the water-carved, oval hole high in the wall on the north side of Tennessee Cove's black cliffs.

Muir Beach Loop

Features: Coastal views, beach

Access: Start at the Tennessee Valley Trailhead. Take the Tennessee Valley and Coastal Trails to Muir Beach. Return via the Green Gulch, Coyote Ridge and Miwok Trails.

Round trip: 8 miles/ moderate-strenuous

Rodeo Beach Loop

Features: Coastal views, wildflowers

Access: Start at the Tennessee Valley trailhead. Take the Tennessee Valley, Chaparral, and Miwok Trails to Rodeo Beach. Return via the Coastal Trail.

Round trip: 6.2 miles/ moderate

Pointers

- Beware of ticks and poison oak.
- If exploring the cove, be careful not to get cut off from the main beach by high tides.
- The water at the beach is too rough, cold, and dangerous for swimming.
- On weekends, be prepared for parking problems.
- A pleasant nearby alternative to the Tennessee Valley crowds is Oakwood Valley, whose wind-protected, gentle floor hosts stands of native Coast Live Oak. Park in the small lot a mile down Tennessee Valley Road.
- Golden Gate Transit buses #10 and #20 both stop at the intersection of Shoreline Highway and Tennessee Valley Road. The stop is within easy walking distance (1.5 miles) of the trailhead.

Elk

When Tennessee Valley was still a part of William A. Richardson's Rancho Saucelito, it harbored wilder animals than today's domestic horses. Once known as Elk Valley, the area was popular for hunting big game such as elk, bear, deer, and wild coyote. As Richardson's son recalled, "Nothing in the world surpassed elk lard to grease a tortilla."

Bicycling

The Tennessee Valley trail offers a leisurely bicycle ride to the beach. Bike racks are provided both halfway down the valley and at the cove. For longer rides, Sausalito and Tiburon bike paths and local roads connect with Tennessee Valley.

Horseback Riding

Tennessee Valley's Miwok Stables provide interpretive guided horseback rides to Muir Beach and other areas. Call for more information.

> **Information:**
> **Marin Headlands**
> **Visitor Center: 331-1540**
> **Miwok Stables: 383-8048**

GGNRA Camping & Overnights

Camping
Marin Headlands   Λ

Hawk Backpack
Location: Hilly backcountry above the Gerbode Valley
Special Features: Bay Area views
Facilities: Campsites, pit toilet, picnic tables, no water, no fires
Access: Hike along Bobcat or Miwok Trail from Rodeo Valley, 3 miles.
Cost: Free
Registration: Reservations and permit required (331-1540).

Haypress Backpack
Location: Grassy, coastal valley north of Tennessee Valley
Special Features: Easy trial backpack for families
Facilities: Campsites, pit toilet, picnic tables, no water, no fires
Access: Hike from Tennessee Valley trailhead and parking lot (no water at lot), 0.75 miles. Access also from Muir Beach, along Coyote Ridge Trail.
Cost: Free
Registration: Reservations and permit required; reserve in advance (331-1540).

Battery Alexander Group Camp
Location: Historic military bunker on coastal headlands south of Rodeo Lagoon
Special Features: Shelter for winter camping
Facilities: Indoor sleeping area in underground bunker, outdoor sleeping area, pit toilets, picnic tables, barbecue grills, water
Access: Drive in from Bunker and Field Roads.
Cost: Free; $25 refundable deposit required.
Registration: Groups only; reservations and permit required. Call 90 days in advance whenever possible (331-1540).

Kirby Cove Group Camp
Location: Picturesque cove and beach at foot of Golden Gate Bridge
Special Features: Bridge and city skyline views
Facilities: Group campsites, tent pads, fire pits, picnic tables, pit toilets, barbecue grills, water
Access: Limited — drive or walk in from Conzelman Road.
Cost: Free
Registration: Groups only; reservations and permit required. Call 90 days in advance (331-1540).

Muir Woods/ Mt.Tamalpais Area   Λ
Pan Toll Campground
Location: Wooded area on flank of Mt. Tamalpais between summit and Muir Woods
Special Features: Access to many superb trails, several to Muir Woods
Facilities: Walk-in tent sites, flush toilets, picnic tables, barbecue grills, water
Access: Hundred-yard walk to tent sites from the parking lot.
Cost: $10/night; $1/night for dogs
Registration: First-come, first-served; no reservations accepted (388-2070).

Shansky Backpack Camp
Location: Pine grove on southwest ridge of Mt. Tamalpais above Muir Woods
Special Features: Good camp spot along the trail from Muir Woods to Muir Beach
Facilities: Group and individual campsites, pit toilets, picnic tables, no water, no open fires
Access: Hike along Coastal Trail from Pan Toll Station, 2 miles.
Cost: $2/per person
Registration: Permit required; reservations recommended in summer (388-2070).

Alice Eastwood Group Camp
Location: Wooded canyon north of Muir Woods
Special Features: Camp among redwoods, many trails
Facilities: Two group campsites (accommodating 25-75 people), pit toilets, barbecue grills, picnic tables, water
Access: Drive or walk in from Panoramic Highway.
Cost: $38-$75 per group site; $3.95 reservation fee per person
Registration: Groups only; reservations and permit required (800/444-7275).

Steep Ravine Environmental Campground
Location: Ocean beach and cove south of Stinson Beach at Rocky Point
Special Features: Beautiful ocean and coastal views
Facilities: Rustic cabins with woodburning stoves, tent sites, pit toilets, picnic tables, barbecue grills, water
Access: Drive in from Highway 1 or hike in on Steep Ravine Trail.
Cost: Cabins $25/night, tent sites $6/night
Registration: Reservations and permit required; for cabins or tent-sites, reserve ten weeks in advance year-round (800/444-7275).

GGNRA North/ Point Reyes   Λ
Glen Camp
Location: Secluded woods between Inverness Ridge and coast in Point Reyes National Seashore
Special Features: Pretty meadow, trees, easy coast access
Facilities: Campsites, picnic tables, pit toilets, barbecue grills, water
Access: Steep 5-mile hike from Five Brooks Trailhead in the Olema Valley along Stewart Trail. Access also from Palomarin or Bear Valley.
Cost: Free
Registration: Reservations and permit necessary; in summer, call 60 days in advance (663-1092, 9-noon weekdays).

Wildcat Camp

Location: Oceanfront cliff north of Double Point in Point Reyes
Special Features: Beach and coastal views
Facilities: Individual and group camp-sites, picnic tables, pit toilets, barbecue grills, water
Access: Steep, 5.7-mile hike from Five Brooks Trailhead in the Olema Valley along the Stewart Trail. Access also from Palomarin and Bear Valley.
Cost: Free
Registration: Reservations and permit required; in summer call 60 days in advance (663-1092).

> *Point Reyes National Seashore has several other campgrounds. Call for more information: 663-1092.*

Olema Ranch Campground

Location: Flat grassland and trees in Olema Valley
Special Features: RV camping
Facilities: RV hook-ups, tent sites, pic-nic tables, showers, flush toilets, laun-dromat, post office, propane, gas, club house, rental trailers
Access: Two miles south of Point Reyes Station on Highway 1
Cost: $15-$20 per night, includes two people; $1/night for dogs
Registration: 8 am-8 pm, reservations recommended in summer (663-8001).

Samuel P. Taylor State Park

Location: Redwood forest on east side of Bolinas Ridge
Special Features: Camp among red-woods.
Facilities: Tent sites, RV sites (no hook-ups), showers, flush toilets, picnic tables, barbecues, water
Access: 15 miles west of San Rafael on Sir Francisco Drake Boulevard
Cost: $10 per night, first vehicle
Registration: Reservations required late April-September (800/444-7275); no reservations rest of the year, first-come, first-served.

American Youth Hostels

San Francisco International Youth Hostel

Location: Upper Fort Mason, San Francisco
Setting: Wooden military building over-looking the Bay
Walk to: GGNRA bayshore, San Francisco, and Golden Gate Bridge
Cost: $10/night
Check-in: 4:30 pm-11 pm (771-7277).

Golden Gate Hostel

Location: Rodeo Valley, Marin Headlands
Setting: Three-story historic house in coastal valley
Walk to: Beach, seacoast fortifications, backcountry
Cost: $7/night
Check-in: 4:30 pm-11 pm. Peak-season shuttle service between Golden Gate and San Francisco Hostel (331-2777).

Point Reyes Hostel

Location: Limantour Beach, Point Reyes National Seashore
Setting: One-story ranch house right on the coast
Walk to: Beach and coastal wilderness trails
Cost: $7/night
Check-in: 4:30-9:30 pm (663-8811).

Hike-in Restaurants and Inns

West Point Inn

Location: Mt. Tamalpais
Description: Pleasant inn with sweep-ing views, veranda, and picnic tables; serves coffee, tea, and lemonade; offers rustic rooms for overnight stays with reservations.
Access: Halfway up Old Railroad Grade between East Peak and Pan Toll Station (388-9955).

Tourist Club

Location: Mt. Tamalpais near Muir Woods
Description: Historic club with deck, picnic tables, and washrooms; serves beer, wine, and soft drinks; offers rooms for overnight stays to club members only.
Access: Hike in from Muir Woods on Panoramic Highway Trail or from the Mountain Home Inn on the Redwood Trail (388-9987).

Mountain Home Inn

Location: Mt. Tamalpais above Muir Woods
Description: Inn with panoramic views and restaurant; serves brunch, lunch, and dinner, as well as beer, wine, and other refreshments; offers rooms for overnight stays with reservations.
Access: Located on Panoramic Highway; hike in from Muir Woods, Muir Beach, Stinson Beach or Mt. Tamalpais trails (381-9000).

Pelican Inn

Location: Muir Beach near Muir Woods
Description: Picturesque inn fashioned after 16th-century English country inn; seven rooms with authentic half-tester beds; serves lunch and dinner of English fare including fish and chips, prime rib, and Yorkshire pudding.
Access: Hike or horse-back ride in from Coastal and other trails; drive in off Highway 1 (383-6000).

Green Gulch Guest House

Location: Green Gulch Farm near Muir Beach
Description: Guest house at Green Gulch Farm — a Buddhist meditation center, organic farm and conference facility; 12 quiet rooms in unique, octag-onal structure built using traditional Japanese joinery; vegetarian meals for overnight guests.
Access: Hike or horse-back ride in from Coastal and other trails; drive in off Highway 1; reservations required (383-3134).

Inns of Point Reyes

Referral and information service: 663-1420.

Adventures in the Park

		Best Locations in GGNRA	Map Page	Area Page
Bike Touring	San Francisco	Lincoln Boulevard	36	40
		Golden Gate Promenade	12	13
		El Camino Del Mar	36	40
	Marin	Stinson Beach Loop	72	84
		Highway 1	54	83
		Olema Valley	88	87
		Bolinas/Fairfax Road	88	85
Birdwatching	San Francisco	Cliff House	36	42
	San Mateo	Sweeney Ridge	50	50
	Marin	Hawk Hill	55	56
		Rodeo Beach & Lagoon	54	62
		Bolinas Lagoon	72	85
		Audubon Canyon Ranch	72	85
Camping	Marin		54, 72	68
Family & Childrens Activities	San Francisco	Hyde Street Pier	13	18
		Fort Mason Center	13	22
	Marin	Rodeo Valley	54	62
		Rocky Point Coast	72	83
Coldwater Swimming	San Francisco	China Beach	37	39
		Aquatic Park	13	18
	Marin	Stinson Beach	72	84
Fishing	San Francisco	Aquatic Park Municipal Pier	13	18
		Fort Mason Piers	13	24
		Fort Point/Crissy Pier	12	26-29
		Baker Beach	37	38
		Ocean Beach	46	47
	Marin	East Fort Baker Pier	55	59
		Tomales Bay	88	92
Hang-Gliding	San Francisco	Fort Funston	46	48
Hiking	San Francisco	Fort Funston	46	48
	San Mateo	Sweeney Ridge	50	50
	Marin	Headlands & backcountry	54	56-69
		Mt. Tam Area & northern parklands	72	74-94
Kayaking	Marin	Sausalito to Kirby Cove	55	56
		Tomales Bay	72	92
Mountain Biking	Marin	Bobcat Trail	55	62-67
		Coyote Ridge Trail	54	81
		Marincello Trail	54	66
		Tennessee Valley Trail	54	66
		Bolinas Ridge Road	88	87
		Lake Lagunitas Loop	72	
		Old Railroad Grade	72	
		Eldridge Grade	72	
Rowing	San Francisco	Aquatic Park	13	18
	Marin	Richardson Bay	55	
Sailing	San Francisco Bay			
Surfing	San Francisco	Fort Point	12	28
		Ocean Beach	46	47
	Marin	Stinson Beach	72	84
		Fort Cronkhite	54	62
Tidepooling	San Mateo	Fitzgerald Marine Preserve		
	Marin	Slide Ranch	73	83
		Duxbury Reef, Bolinas	88	85
Volunteer Work	San Francisco & Marin			
Windsurfing	San Francisco	Crissy Field	12	26
	Marin	Stinson Beach	72	84
		Tomales Bay	72	92
Whale Watching	Marin	Muir Beach Overlook	73	82
		Point Reyes Lighthouse		94
		Gulf of the Farallones	4	82

Equipment Rentals* & Organized Activities

Tips

Marin Cyclists, P.O.Box 2611,
   San Rafael, CA 94912
Park Cyclery (SF)* 221-3777
Sausalito Cyclists* 332-3050
Sierra Club 653-6127

- Be prepared for weekend car traffic.
- Always carry an extra innertube, so
  you're trip doesn't end in the woods.
- Watch out for people on foot.

Audubon Society.............383-1770 & 388-2524
Audubon Canyon Ranch 868-9244
Golden Gate Raptor Observatory 331-0730
Sierra Club 653-6127

- Best hawkwatching spot is Hawk Hill
  in the Marin Headlands, best season is fall.
- Audubon Canyon Ranch hosts thriving heron
  and egret rookeries.
- Please do not disturb the birds.

National Park Service 331-1540
Sierra Club 653-6127

- See p. 68 for comprehensive information on
  camping and overnight stays parkwide.

Family Farm Days at Slide Ranch 381-6155
Headlands Inst. Env.Ed. Camp 332-5771
Ocean Alliance Sea & Sail Camp 441-5970
Chantey singalongs / Hyde St. Pier ...556-1871
Terwilliger Nature Ed. Center 927-1670

Dolphin Swim & Boating Club 441-9329
South End Swim & Rowing Club 776-7372
Stinson Beach Weather 868-1922

- Bay water temperatures range from 51-60 F;
  average Stinson water temperature is 58 F.
- China Beach lifeguards on duty April-October.
- Stinson Beach lifeguards on duty May-October.
- September offers the warmest H_2O temperatures.

California Fish & Game Dept. ...(707) 944-5500
Salty Lady Sport Fishing 348-2107
Wacky Jacky fishing expeditions 586-9800

- Regional waters are renowned for good salmon
  fishing.
- Please observe California Fish & Game regulations
  regarding catch size and take.

Chandelle Hang-Gliding Center 359-6800
Fellow Feathers Club 641-5680

- Fort Funston, a Hang III intermediate site, is
  world renowned for its hang-gliding conditions.
- Viewing deck on-site for those who prefer to watch.
  Fort Funston conditions 333-0100

Golden Gate National Park Assoc. 556-0693
NPS Ranger-led hikes 556-0560
   (and all site information numbers)

- Pick up *Park Events* at all visitor centers. This
  calendar describes ranger programs throughout
  the GGNRA.

Bay Area Sea Kayakers 457-6094
Sea Trek...332-4457

- Best put-in spots:
  Crissy Field; Schoonmaker Point Marina Beach in
  Sausalito; Muir Beach; Heart's Desire Beach and
  Nick's Cove on Tomales Bay.
- Check tides to plan trips.
- Usually less windy in mornings.
- Tomales Bay conditions...............................669-1140

Marin Bicycle Trails Council 472-2453
Wombats, P.O.Box 757, Fairfax, CA 94930

- Bring water!
- Please be considerate of hikers, walkers
  and other trail users.
- Check with local rangers on current mountain
  biking regulations before setting off.

Dolpin Swim & Boating Club 441-9329
Marin Rowing Association 461-1431
Open Water Rowing............................332-1091

- Best put-in spots:
  Aquatic Park; Schoonmaker Point Marina Beach,
  Sausalito.

Dave Garrett Sailing 331-3364
Ocean Alliance 441-5970
S.F.— Sausalito Sailing Club 331-6266

- An unusual and spectacular way to enjoy
  parklands from offshore.

Double Overhead Association 665-7745

- Beware of strong currents and rip tides;
  if you get caught, go with the flow.
- Stinson Beach surf report 868-1922
- General surf report 726-9283

Duxbury Reef, write for schedule: Marin Co
   Parks, Civic Center, San Rafael, CA 94905.....
Fitzgerald Marine Preserve 728-3584
Slide Ranch 381-6155
Sierra Club 653-6127

- Low tide is the best time for tidepooling.
- Beware of sneaker waves and rising tides.
- Please do not remove anemones, seastars or tidal life.
- Tide tables from: Ocean Alliance 441-5970
  Gulf of the Farallones NMS 556-3509

General volunteer info.....556-3535 or 556-0693
Habitat Restoration Team 556-0693
Hawk Watch volunteers......................331-0730
Historic Ships work parties 332-8409

- The National Park Service and the many non-profit
  organizations in the GGNRA offer a wide variety
  of exciting positions for volunteers.

Cityfront Sailboards* 929-7873
S.F. Board Sailing Association,
   2174 Union St., Box 47, S.F., CA 94123

- Crissy Field is the best windsurfing/board-sailing
  launch site on the Bay.
- The afternoon is best for favorable northwest winds.

Ocean Alliance 474-3385

- Gray whales most visible December-April.

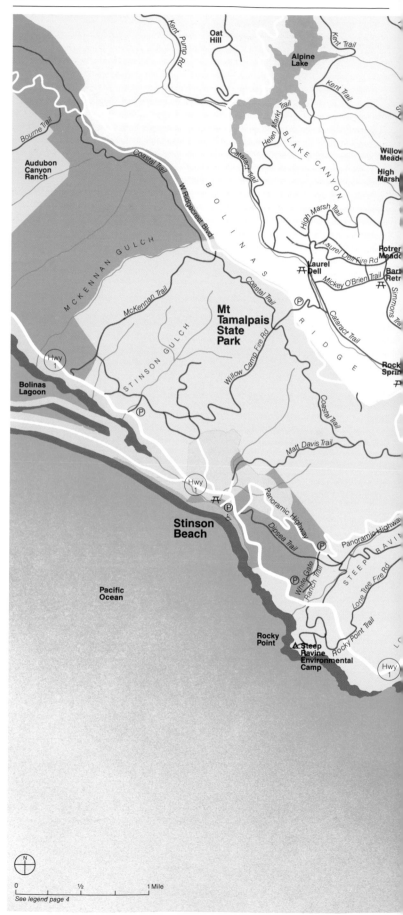

Oat Hill

Kent Pump Rd

Kent Trail

Alpine Lake

Kent Trail

Helen Markt Trail

Cataract Trail

B L A K E   C A N Y O N

Willow Mead

High Marsh

High Marsh Trail

Bourne Trail

Coastal Trail

Audubon Canyon Ranch

W Ridgecrest Blvd

B O L I N A S

Laurel Dell Fire Rd

Potrer Mead

Laurel Dell

Mickey O'Brien Trail

Bart Retr

M C K E N N A N   G U L C H

McKennan Trail

S T I N S O N   G U L C H

Mt Tamalpais State Park

Coastal Trail

Willow Camp Fire Rd

Cataract Trail

R I D G E

Simmons Tra

Rock Sprin

Hwy 1

Bolinas Lagoon

Coastal Trail

Matt Davis Trail

Stinson Beach

Hwy 1

Panoramic Highway

Dipsea Trail

Panoramic Highwa

S T E E P   R A V I N

Pacific Ocean

White Gate Ranch Trail

Lone Tree Fire Rd

Rocky Point

Steep Ravine Environmental Camp

Rocky Point Trail

L O

Hwy 1

N

0   ½   1 Mile

See legend page 4

Bon Tempe Lake

Lagunitas Picnic

Pilot Knob

Lake Lagunitas

Lakeview Rd

Kentfield

Stocking Trail

Berry Trail

Collier Springs Trail

Tucker Trail

Rock Springs-Lagunitas Trail

Bay Tree Junction

Eldridge Trail

Tucker Trail

Indian Fire Rd

Lower North Side Trail

Inspiration Point

Temelpa Trail

North Side Trail

Echo Rock

Corte Madera

entine

oon Rd

Azalea Flat

Upper North Side Trail

Side Trail

International Trail

MOUNT TAMALPAIS

Middle Peak 2490'

East Peak 2571'

Verna Dunshee

Gardener Lookout

Indian Trail

Wheeler Trail

Hoo-Koo-E-Koo Rd

Rifle Camp Site

Arturo Trail

West Peak 2560'

Fern Creek

Miller Trail

Telephone Trail

Summit Ave

ings-Lagunitas

E Ridgecrest Blvd

Alice Eastwood Trail

Old Stage Rd

Old Railroad Grade

Grade Trail

Hoo-Koo-E-Koo Rd

Old Railroad Grade

Rock Springs Trail

Nora Trail

West Point Inn

Matt Davis Trail

Panoramic Hwy

Cascade Dr

Mountain Theater

Bootjack Trail

Easy Grade Trail

Old Mine Trail

Matt Davis Trail

Troop 80 Trail

Bootjack

Sierra Trail

Gravity Car Grade

Mountain Home Inn

Zig-Zag Trail

Old Pipeline Trail

Panoramic Trail

Tenderfoot Trail

Mill Valley

Edgewood Rd

Van Wyck Meadow

Camp Eastwood Rd

Alice Eastwood Group Camp

Camp Eastwood Fire Rd

Lost Trail

Pantoll Ranger Station

TCC Trail

REDWOOD CANYON

Bootjack Trail

Kent Memorial

Panoramic Hwy Trail

Redwood Trail

Tourist Club

Sequoia Valley Rd

p Ravine Trail

Old Mine Trail

Ben Johnson Trail

Hillside Trail

Muir Woods National Monument

Sun Trail

sea Trail

Stapelveldt Trail

Dipsea Trail

KENT CANYON

Deer Park Fire Rd

Visitor Center

Muir Woods Rd

Dipsea Trail

YON

Coastal Trail Fire Rd

Mt. Tamalpais State Park

GULCH

Shansky Backpack

COLD STREAM CANYON

Frank Valley Cutoff

Redwood Creek Trail

FRANK VALLEY

Muir Woods Rd

Miwok Trail

Hwy

Heather Cutoff

Slide Ranch

Dias Ridge Rd

DIAZ RIDGE

Hwy 1

Pelican Inn

Zen Center Green Gulch Farm

Green Gulch Trail

GREEN GULCH

Muir Beach Overlook

Coyote Ridge Trail

Muir Beach

Coastal Trail

Muir Woods

Walking
Redwoods
Visitor information
Hiking

Awalk through Muir Woods is a meeting with what one botanist called "a Titan race." The world's most famous grove of virgin redwoods grows in a cool, foggy canyon north of the Golden Gate. These tall trees are a spectacular remnant of the vast redwood forests which once surrounded San Francisco Bay. Easy, paved trails loop through Muir Woods along a creek where salmon spawn each winter. Black-tail deer, grey squirrels, and other wild creatures roam among the majestic redwoods — once referred to by German architect Eric Mendelsohn as "God's own flagpoles."

The Visitor Center

The visitor center at the entrance to the Woods has exhibits and an excellent selection of brochures, books, and other information on Muir Woods.

The Redwoods

At Muir Woods, the average age of the redwoods ranges from 400 to 800 years old; one ancient specimen has been around for 12 centuries. The tallest coast redwood in the grove stands 253 feet high. *Sequoia sempervirens* is the tallest of the world's tree species. It thrives in the cool, moist, foggy climate near the coast. Young trees grow from tiny seeds in small cones or sprout from old snags or roots.

The Creek

Redwood Creek brings the magic of rushing rapids and quiet pools to Muir Woods. Four footbridges cross the creek, perfect spots to watch water skippers, crayfish, salmon, and steelhead in the water.

Seasonal Flora and Fauna

Winter
Spawning salmon, varied thrushes (orange and black) banana slugs, mushrooms, other fungus (honey and oyster mushrooms)

Spring
Wildflowers (milkmaid, azaleas, starflower, wild ginger, miner's lettuce, violets, iris, trillium)

Summer
Deer (does and fawns), chipmunks, steller's jays, baby salmon, steelhead, clustering ladybugs

Fall
Monarch butterflies, deer (bucks and does), fall color

"This is their temple,
vaulted high,
And here we pause
with reverent eye,
With silent tongue and
awe-struck soul;
For here we sense life's
proper goal;
To be like them,
straight, true and fine,
To make our world,
like theirs, a shrine;
Sink down, oh, trav-
eller, on your knees,
God stands before you
in these trees."

Joseph B. Strauss, Builder of
the Golden Gate Bridge

Trails

Muir Woods visitors can take an easy loop on the forest floor or strike out for longer hikes on a variety of trails (see map pp. 72-73). The gentle, paved main trails through Muir Woods are easy going in any kind of footwear; all are wheelchair and stroller accessible. Longer hikes include:

Redwood Groves Loop

Features: Get away from crowds, views overlooking redwoods and creek

Access: Walk through woods and cross fourth bridge. Take the Hillside Trail to the left and back to entrance.

Round trip: 2 miles/ easy

Fern Creek Loop

Features: Creek, canyon views, picnic spot, no crowds

Access: Walk through Muir Woods past third bridge. Take the Fern Creek Trail to Alice Eastwood Camp. Return

down via the Bootjack Spur fire road and Bootjack Trail.

Round trip: 4 miles/ moderate

Ben Johnson Loop

Features: Spectacular views, picnic spots, redwoods, no crowds

Access: Walk through Muir Woods and cross fourth bridge. Take the Ben Johnson Trail up and return via the Dipsea Trail.

Round trip: 4.5 miles/moderate

Dipsea Loop

Features: Varied scenery, spectacular views, creek, sun, shade

Access: Cross the Dipsea bridge at lower parking lot of Muir Woods and take the Dipsea and TCC trails to the Bootjack Picnic Area. Return via the Bootjack Trail.

Round trip: 8.5 miles/ strenuous

Hassle-Free Loop

Features: Vistas, redwoods, wildflowers, refreshments, no parking problems

Access: Start at the Mountain Home Inn on the Panoramic Highway. Take the Panoramic Trail (Oceanview Trail) to the Panoramic Highway Trail to the Lost Trail to the Fern Creek Trail and down through Muir Woods. Return via the Panoramic Highway Trail.

Round trip: 4.5 miles/ moderate

Frank Valley

Features: Creek, beach, connections to coastal trails

Access: Start at the junction of Frank Valley Road and Deer Park Fire Road. Take the Redwood Creek Trail west to Muir Beach and other trailheads.

One way: 2.5 miles/ easy

Salmon Spawning in Redwood Creek

Heavy winter rains break open the sandbar at the mouth of Redwood Creek, sending a stream of fresh water into the Pacific Ocean. The sudden surge of fresh water tells the salmon out in the ocean that it's time to return to the stream of their birth to spawn. Fighting their way up the rocky bounds and twists of the creek, the fish arrive battered and exhausted at Muir Woods two or three days later. It's easy to see the spawning rituals of the bright, brick-red salmon from the footbridges among the redwoods.

First, the male courts the female, chasing other suitors away. Then, the female digs a hollow in the gravel — a redd — and lays eggs. After the male fertilizes the eggs and the female covers them up, the salmon swim listlessly around the pools and shallows of the creek until they die. To see the biggest spawning runs wait two or three days after a big winter storm in January, February, or March. Steelhead trout also spawn in the creek in early spring.

The Saving of Muir Woods

John Muir

Back in Gold Rush times, local forests were being felled right and left in order to build homes, shops, and other facilities for the thousands of people who suddenly descended upon San Francisco. Due to its inaccessibility, Muir Woods escaped the saw until 1905 when lumber businessmen laid plans to cut it down. Luckily, Marin County conservationist and politician William Kent bought the canyon to save these last redwoods. Even with Kent's purchase, however, Muir Woods was still in danger. Two years later, a local water company sued to condemn the canyon floor for a reservoir. Kent sent a desperate plea for help to President Theodore Roosevelt. Enchanted with Kent's photographs of the slender giants, Roosevelt agreed to declare the canyon a national monument.

When John Muir heard of Kent's great deed, he said, "This is the best tree-lovers' monument that could be found in all the forests of the world. Saving these redwoods from the axe and saw, from money changers and water changers, is, in many ways, the most notable service to God and man I have heard since my forest wanderings began..." It was at Kent's special request that the forest was named after Muir.

William Kent

Ladybugs in the Woods

Every May, thousands of ladybugs migrate from California's hot Central Valley to cool, coastal areas such as Muir Woods. Clouds of these tiny, bright-red insects swarm and hover among the redwoods during the summer. On cool days, they cluster together to conserve body heat, hanging from branches and shrubs in partial hibernation.

Fire

Before settlers came to the Bay Area, massive fires burned through the region's forests every 20 to 50 years. Fire has always been a part of the GGNRA landscape, whether kindled by storms or by the Indians who used fire to increase seed yields, drive game, and improve visibility for hunting. In the forest, fire actually serves as a natural cleansing agent, clearing out deadwood, killing pests, fertilizing the soil, and giving new plants a chance to grow. Many a fire-blackened hollow marks the tree trunks at Muir Woods.

Pointers

◆ The best time to visit is weekdays, or early or late on weekend days. Summer weekends are very crowded.

◆ A nice way to avoid parking problems is to hike in from other park areas.

◆ Dress warmly; it's always cool among the redwoods.

◆ For picnickers, dog walkers, and late nighters, Homestead Valley is a great place to go. The valley, adjacent to Muir Woods, stays open 24 hours a day. It's especially suitable for flying model airplanes and star-gazing away from city lights. Other good spots for picnicking are Muir Beach and Muir Beach Overlook.

◆ Golden Gate Transit bus #63 stops on the Panoramic Highway at the Mountain Home Inn, Pan Toll, and other Muir Woods trailheads. From these access points, it's an easy downhill hike to the Woods. Bus service on weekends and holidays only.

Information:
388-2595

Mt. Tamalpais

Hiking
Picnicking
Camping
Visitor information

O n a crystal-clear day, hikers at the top of Mt. Tamalpais can see the Sierra Nevada 200 miles away. These faraway peaks are only one of the magnificent and panoramic views from Marin's highest mountain — other views include Tiburon, Mt. Diablo, the Marin Headlands, the Pacific Ocean, the Farallon Islands, and, of course, the Financial District scraping San Francisco's skies. No wonder Mt. Tamalpais has been popular Bay Area hiking turf since the 1880s. Some of the region's most well-trodden trails traverse "Mt. Tam," dipping into redwood valleys, winding across open grasslands, and following ridge lines from summit to coast.

Pan Toll Ranger Station

The Pan Toll ranger station, located off the Panoramic Highway, is a good place to get hiking and camping maps and information. Though most of Mt. Tam lies within the legislated boundaries of the GGNRA, the mountain is largely managed by Mt. Tamalpais State Park and the Marin Municipal Water District.

Picnic Areas

There are two drive-in picnic areas on Mt. Tam. Bootjack Picnic Area is located at a pleasant, wooded, and shady site off the Panoramic Highway just east of Pan Toll. It has barbecues, picnic tables, rest rooms, and running water. The East Peak Picnic Area lies in a sunny and shady site at the end of East Ridgecrest Boulevard. It offers the same picnicking facilities as Bootjack except the barbecues. No fires are allowed at East Peak.

The Ridge Road

The 20-minute drive along West Ridgecrest Boulevard down the northern flank of Mt. Tam affords splendid views from dazzling heights above GGNRA's coast. It's a great road for a sunset drive when the fog is out; when it's in, visitors often find themselves high up over the mist in clear skies. West Ridgecrest Boulevard runs for four miles between Rock Springs and the Bolinas/Fairfax Road. (On some maps it appears incorrectly as Bolinas Ridge Road.)

Manzanita

Mt. Tam Visitor Center

At the summit of East Peak is a small visitor center which displays exhibits on local plants, animals, and geology, as well as historic maps of the area. The center, located off East Ridgecrest Boulevard, is usually open on weekends.

Footprint of Raccoon

Waterfall Trails

In the springtime, water flows down Mt. Tam and through GGNRA's surrounding parklands in torrents — producing many small, but exquisite, waterfalls. Trails offering the best waterfall views are: Steep Ravine, Troop 80 and the Cataract Trail (see map pp. 72-73).

Mt. Tamalapis

> *"Brave Tamalpais! he
> looks so grand,
> Bluffing the oceans
> off, guarding the
> land."*
> Charles Warren Stoddard

Trails

*Combined with the adjacent GGNRA and Marin Municipal Water District,
the Mt. Tamalpais area offers over 200 miles of hiking trails. Here are a few
favorite hikes. See map on pp. 72-73 for trail locations.*

Verna Dunshee Loop

Features: Best Mt. Tam vista point

Access: Start at East Peak parking lot. Follow paved loop counter-clockwise around peak.

Round trip: 0.7 miles/ easy

Steep Ravine Loop

Features: Views, waterfalls, redwood canyon

Access: Start at Pan Toll. Take the Old Mine Trail down to the Dipsea Trail. Follow the Dipsea to Webb Creek. Return via the Steep Ravine Trail.

Round trip: 3.5 miles/ strenuous (1,100 ft. elevation change)

Old Mine Trail

Features: S.F skyline views, woods, grasslands, picnic spot

Access: Start at Pan Toll. Take the Old Mine Trail down to the scenic grassy outcrop near the junction with the Dipsea Trail.

One way: 0.5 miles/ easy

Muir Woods Loop

Features: Creek, fir and redwood forests

Access: Start at Pan Toll. Take the Alpine and Bootjack Trails to Muir Woods. Return via the Ben Johnson and Staplevelt Trails.

Round trip: 4 miles/ strenuous (1,200 ft. elevation change)

Matt Davis Hike-down/Ride-up Loop

Features: Coastal views, fir forests, beach

Access: Start at Pan Toll station. Take the Matt Davis Trail down to Stinson Beach. Return via Golden Gate Transit bus #63.

One way: 3.7 miles/ easy

Laurel Dell Loop

Features: Wildflowers, views, picnic area

Access: Start at Pan Toll. Take the Matt Davis, Coastal, and Willow Camp Fire Road Trails to West Ridgecrest Boulevard. Cross and continue on Laurel Dell Fire Road to the picnic area. Return via the Cataract Trail to Rock Springs and down the Old Mine Trail.

Round trip: 6 miles/ moderate

The Crookedest Railroad

Mt. Tamalpais enjoys the unique distinction of having once had the world's crookedest railroad scale its southern slope. Built in 1896, the Mill Valley and Mt. Tamalpais Scenic Railroad negotiated 281 hairpin curves on its eight-mile way to the summit. Everyone loved the railroad. In its heyday, the railroad's logging-type, Shay steam locomotives pushed 50,000 passengers a year up the mountain in canopied cars. In 1907, the railroad added another thrill, a gravity glide to Muir Woods. Riders came from near and far to try out this new branch

line, which later became known as the "longest roller-coaster ride in the world." The day came, however, when the automobile arrived and drove all the railroad's passengers away. The tracks of the Mill Valley and Mt. Tamalpais Scenic Railroad were removed in the 1930s. Visitors can hike the Old Railroad Grade Trail from the north side of the Mountain Home Inn to Blithedale Ridge in Mill Valley.

The Mountain Theater

During the early 1900s, people gathered in a grassy meadow 2,000 feet up the side of Mt. Tam to see outdoor plays. Later, the New Deal's Civilian Conservation Corps improved this natural amphitheater by installing stone seats, leveling the stage, and landscaping the site. Today, this mountainside spot still serves as a stage for plays, concerts, and special events.

The Dipsea Race

The Dipsea Race is an arduous 7.1-mile run which begins in Mill Valley, climbs over a ridge of Mt. Tam, passes through Muir Woods, and descends to Stinson Beach. This venerable race has been held every year since 1905, and today attracts over 1,500 runners.

Tiny Trees — A Forest of Dwarf Cypress

Out on Mt. Tam's slopes grow some mighty small cypress trees. The lack of nutrients in the serpentine soil stunts the growth of the cypress so they mature when only a few feet tall. To visit this pygmy cypress forest, take either the Benstein Trail north from Rock Springs or the Old Stage Road half a mile northeast of the Bootjack Picnic Area.

Plant Communities on Mt. Tam

Coastal Scrub	Oak Woodland	Prairie	Chaparral	Redwood and Douglas Fir Forest
Coyote Brush	Oak	Native California Grass	Chemise	
Sage	Bay	Mediterranean Grass	Manzanita	
Lupine	Buckeye	Hotter and dryer	Ceanothus	
Generally at lower elevations in fog zones	Madrone	above fog line		

Pointers

◆ For more detailed information and maps of specific hikes on Mt. Tamalpais, try Dan and Kay Martin's *Mt. Tam, a hiking, running and nature guide.*

◆ During hot weather, parts of Mt. Tamalpais are sometimes closed due to fire danger. For an update, call Pan Toll.

◆ For camping information, see pp. 68-69.

◆ Visitors in search of refreshments will find them at the Mountain Home Inn, the West Point Inn, and the Tourist Club (see pp. 68-69).

◆ Trails cross many boundaries, traversing the state park, the water district, and the GGNRA.

◆ Check for dog restrictions before bringing one along.

◆ Golden Gate Transit bus #63 runs from Stinson Beach up to Pan Toll Station and along the Panoramic Highway, stopping at many mountain trailheads. Weekends and holidays only.

Information:

Pan Toll: 388-2070

Mountain Theater (Mountain Play): 383-1100

Muir Beach

Beachcombing
Birdwatching
Sunbathing
Picnicking
Fishing
Dog walking

Often less crowded than neighboring Stinson, Muir Beach offers a quiet spot for seaside recreation three miles west of Muir Woods. Sunbathers can brave the crisp Pacific breeze; fish freaks can watch the salmon work their way upstream to spawn; hikers can picnic on their way north or south over the coastal bluffs; butterfly enthusiasts can marvel at the Monarchs wintering in a nearby pine grove.

The Beach and Lagoon

The Muir Beach sandbar traps some of the out-flowing water from Redwood Creek in a lagoon. Visitors to this small but lovely beach can either splash in the cool ocean surf or wade in the warm calm of the lagoon.

Salt Grass which grows in lagoons and other wetlands

Monarch Butterflies

Every autumn, thousands of Monarch butterflies embark on a once-in-a-lifetime migration to the California coast. A tagged Monarch recently set a migration distance record — flying 660 miles from Santa Barbara to southeastern Arizona in five months. The grove of Monterey pine at Muir Beach is one site where these orange and black butterflies spend the winter.

Coastal Hikes

Beyond the lagoon, a green gate leads to the Coastal Trail. Hikers can go east along the trail (uphill) to scenic Coyote Ridge or south to Tennessee Cove.

The Picnic Area

The sheltered picnic area next to Muir Beach Lagoon is furnished with barbecue grills, tables, rest rooms, and a changing area.

The Franciscan Formation

For geology buffs, Pirate's Cove on the Coastal Trail between Muir Beach and Tennessee Valley offers fine, isolated outcrops of Franciscan Formation rocks. The formation, which underlies large areas of the GGNRA, is a melange of sandstones, shales, chert, basalt and other rocks from the ocean bottom. These long-submerged rocks were caught in the middle as the seafloor slowly slid under the North American geologic plate millions of years ago. Geologists named this local jumble of deep-sea rocks the Franciscan Formation after San Francisco.

Pointers

♦ Muir Beach is a nice place to picnic after a trip to Muir Woods.

♦ Be prepared for crowds on weekends.

♦ The Pelican Inn offers refreshments, meals, and overnight accommodations (see pp. 68-69).

Information:
388-2595

Muir Beach Overlook

Vistas
Picnicking
Whale watching

A small signpost north of Muir Beach along Highway 1 points the way to Muir Beach Overlook. The clear views from this high, coastal bluff led military planners to site several base-end stations there long ago. Though no one searches for enemy ships from the site today, visitors to Muir Beach Overlook can explore the old stations, hike to the tip of a rocky promontory, and enjoy views of migrating whales and the California coastline.

The Overlook Trail

The short but breathtaking overlook trail follows the narrow crest of a coastal promontory. On either side of the promontory, the terrain sheers off dramatically down to the ocean hundreds of feet below.

Whale Watching

Muir Beach Overlook is just one of the many spots along GGNRA's coast where whale lovers can watch these giant marine mammals swim by during their winter migrations. Between the overlook and the Farallon Islands sweeps the Gulf of the Farallones, an ocean region full of dolphins, porpoises, seals, and whales. Indeed, these normally rare sea creatures are so abundant in the Gulf that the region now enjoys federal protection in the form of the 948-square-nautical-mile Gulf of the Farallones National Marine Sanctuary.

Gray Whale
Length: 30-45 feet
Color: Gray, mottled
Local Habitat: Gulf of the Farallones
Migration Season: November-June
Most Visible: December-April
Calving Grounds: Lagoons in Baja California, Mexico

Base-End Stations

Before the invention of radar, soldiers here calculated the range of approaching ships by sight, measuring the angle of view between their station and the ship. Based on angles reported from different locations, the distance, speed, and direction of the target ship could be calculated.

Pointers

♦ The overlook picnic site is scenic but windy, so come prepared to batten down the paper plates.

♦ Those with a fear of heights should avoid the overlook trail.

♦ For whale-watching trips, call the Oceanic Society.

Information:
388-2595

Oceanic Society whale watch: 474-3385

National Marine Sanctuary: 556-3509

Rocky Point Coast

Hiking
Fishing
Camping
Tidepooling

Between Muir Beach and Stinson Beach lie several miles of the views and vistas that make California so famous — spectacular rocky reefs, rugged headlands, and the Pacific surf. The best spots for a visit to this stretch of coast are the Steep Ravine beach and the tidepools of Slide Ranch.

Tidepooling and Farming at Slide Ranch

Two miles north of Muir Beach on Highway 1, an unassuming driveway leads to Slide Ranch. This small demonstration farm and environmental education center is also one of five major tidepooling spots in the Bay Area.

For those who prefer goats and chickens to tidepool life, Slide Ranch offers environmental and farm education programs between February and November.

Steep Ravine

Steep Ravine descends from Mt. Tam to the Rocky Point coast, ending in the Pacific surf with a small, sandy beach. Visitors can hike down to the beach from the sign-posted gate on Highway 1, two miles south of Stinson. On the other side of Highway 1, the Steep Ravine Trail climbs up a lush, narrow canyon filled with redwoods and waterfalls to Pan Toll Station. In addition, visitors can stay the night in one of Steep Ravine's ocean-front cabins or campsites (reservations required; see pp. 68-69).

The Intertidal Zone

Slide Ranch's tidepools are part of GGNRA's extensive intertidal zone, one filled with urchins, anemones, seastars, and other fascinating creatures. As the tides rise and fall, intertidal organisms are exposed to pounding waves, hot sun, and constantly changing temperatures and salinity levels. Many organisms have developed special adaptations to help them survive these challenging conditions — fastening onto rocks, burrowing into cracks, or covering up with shells and pebbles. Among the rarest tidepool creatures are sea slugs. These *nudibranchs* are no short, fat, slimy worms, but the ocean's equivalent of butterflies. The best times to see these amazing and exquisite creatures are summer and fall.

Scenic Highway 1

Those in search of a pretty drive along GGNRA's shoreline can take Highway 1 all the way from Mill Valley to Point Reyes. Rocky Point is one of the many scenic areas of rugged coastline along the way.

Pointers

♦ The cliffs along the Rocky Point coast are isolated and very dangerous, so please be careful. Rescue crews are far away.

Information:
Ranger Station: 868-0942
Slide Ranch: 381-6155

Stinson Beach

Swimming
Surfing
Sunbathing
Picnicking
Volleyball

S tinson Beach has been a favorite bathing spot for local residents since the turn of the century. Stinson's miles of white sand and oceanfront make it one of the best swimming beaches in northern California, not to mention a favorite surfing, picnicking, and volleyball spot. Whatever the activity, Stinson offers visitors complete water recreation facilities and services.

The Beach

Stinson Beach is a three-mile-long sandbar completely free of rocks. It's a place to walk for miles on white sand, take a dip, have a barbecue, jog, or play games on the beach. Visitors can even borrow volleyball nets and balls from the main lifeguard tower in exchange for a driver's license. Lifeguards are on duty May through October. The average summer water temperature is 58 degrees Fahrenheit.

The Picnic Area

Stinson Beach has an extensive picnic area with tables and barbecues. For those who forget their picnic baskets, there's a snack bar at the base of the main lifeguard tower.

The Surf

Stinson Beach is popular for board and windsurfing, rafting, and boogie-boarding. For surfers, the best times of year are winter and spring when storms give the beach a steeper face and more uneven bottom. For wind-  surfers, the prevailing northwesterly winds blow best in the afternoon. For rafters and boogie-board users, the summer surf is most suitable.

Rip Currents

What's popularly called an undertow is really a rip current. Rip currents are caused by wave action pushing water up the beach and then rushing back down the narrow channels between offshore sand bars. At Stinson Beach, rip currents occur year-round and can carry swimmers hundreds of yards from shore. Look for the informational warning displays posted at the beach.

The Town

The adjacent town of Stinson Beach offers several restaurants, a small grocery store, and a handful of shops.

Pointers

- Visit during non-peak hours.
- On hot days, the parking lot often fills by 11 a.m. There is no place else to park, so please call for an update on the parking situation before setting off.
- Golden Gate Transit bus #63 runs from Highway 101 along the Panoramic Highway to Stinson Beach on weekends and holidays.

Information:
Ranger Station: 868-0942
Surf and parking report: 868-1922

Stinson Beach and Bolinas Lagoon

Bolinas Lagoon

**Walking
Birdwatching
Wildlife**

Bolinas Lagoon's diverse wildlife, pristine marshes, and water-snaked mud flats make it one of the richest wetlands on GGNRA's shores. This birdwatcher's paradise is bordered by the seaside village of Bolinas, Highway 1, and the Stinson Beach sandbar.

Great Egret

Birds, Seals, and Lagoon Life

There's always wildlife to be seen at Bolinas Lagoon. Snowy egrets, blackbirds, warblers, and dozens of other bird and animal species live in and around this County Wildlife Preserve. Some of the seasonal wildlife highlights include ducks in the winter, herons in the spring, pelicans in the summer, and sparrows in the fall. Between April and June, harbor seals and their pups often appear on Pickleweed Island.

Trails & Overlooks

Wildlife can easily be seen from the roadside pulloffs along the lagoon on Highway 1.

Trails: Park near the Bolinas Nursery on the lagoon side of the Bolinas/Olema Road. Walk back toward the Highway 1 junction. Just beyond the sharp corner, a trail sets off across the lagoon through a hole in the fence near a county preserve sign. Those who miss that trailhead can also enter the lagoon where the fence ends.

Scenic Lagoon Overlook: Take the Bolinas/Fairfax Road up (east) from Highway 1 about one mile to where the road takes a sharp curve to the left. Park, climb over the gate on the left, and walk through the open meadow toward the lagoon for a beautiful view and picnic area.

Birdwatching at Audubon Canyon Ranch

Audubon Canyon Ranch is a nonprofit, private, thousand-acre wildlife sanctuary and nature education center on Bolinas Lagoon. During the spring, over a hundred pairs of Great Egrets and Great Blue Herons nest in the tops of the ranch's redwoods. The adjacent lagoon provides these wading and fishing birds with ample food for their young. The nestlings hatch in May and June — the best time for a visit to Audubon Canyon Ranch. Several miles of ranch trails are open to the public mid-March through mid-July, including the 0.75-mile, self-guided Harwell Nature Trail; the Bourne Trail which climbs 1,400 feet to Bolinas Ridge; and the Kent and Rawlings Trails which lead to the rookery overlook. Visitors can pick up a trail map at the ranch. Limited visiting hours.

Great Blue Heron	Great Egret
Height: 4-5 feet	**Height:** 3.5-4 feet
Wingspan: 6 feet	**Wingspan:** 4.5 feet
Color: Blue and grey	**Color:** White
Arrive at Ranch: January	**Arrive at Ranch:** Mid-March
Number of Eggs: 2-5	**Number of Eggs:** 2-5
Young fly after: 9 weeks	**Young fly after:** 7 weeks

Great Blue Heron

Harbor Seals

Bolinas Lagoon visitors looking out from Highway 1 can easily see the harbor seals hauled out on Pickleweed and Kent Islands, and on the lagoon's tidal sandbars. Harbor seals have a physiological need to come on shore (haul-out) almost daily to rest. They also haul-out to give birth and rear their young during the pupping season. Though Bolinas Lagoon is not a major breeding area, visitors can often see 150 or more seals and their pups at the lagoon's haul-out spots. The best seal watching months are April through June. Apart from their smaller size, torpedo shape, and stubby flippers, harbor seals differ from sea lions in two ways: On land, they walk inchworm fashion, unlike sea lions who progress on all fours; and their ears lack the external ear pinna seen in sea lions. The characteristics given below are for adult harbor seals.

Harbor Seals
Color: Black, light brown, and white.
Characteristics: Spotted
Length: 4-5 feet
Weight: 200-250 pounds
Average Age: 20 years
Appear: Year-round

Invertebrate Life in the Mud

A muddy lagoon awash with freshwater runoff and salt water tides may seem an uncomfortable sort of place to live. Yet a hardy group of organisms called invertebrates thrives in the ooze. These tiny, spineless shrimps, worms, and other creatures can regulate their body salt levels to accommodate the constant changes in salinity. The presence of invertebrates is one reason why estuaries are one of the most productive ecosystems on the planet.

Flowering Peanut Worm

Pointers

◆ In the summer, lagoon walkers can get away with regular walking boots. In the winter and spring, rubber boots are recommended.

◆ Please do not disturb the seals or birds.

◆ For a quarterly schedule of lagoon walks led by the county naturalist, write to Marin County Parks and Open Space Department, Civic Center, San Rafael, CA 94903.

◆ There are no road signs for Bolinas, so use the map for orientation.

◆ For a ridgetop hike overlooking the whole region, see section on Bolinas and Inverness Ridge Trails (p. 89).

Information:
Ranger Station: 868-0942
Audubon Canyon Ranch: 868-9244
Marin County Parks: 499-6387

Great Egrets in Bolinas Lagoon

Olema Valley

Hiking
Camping
Horseback riding
Mountain biking

razing cattle and Victorian farms instill the Olema Valley with a soft, rural charm. This pastoral landscape stretches for nine miles between the dark slopes of Bolinas and Inverness Ridges. The border between the GGNRA and Point Reyes National Seashore meanders along the valley floor, enabling Olema visitors to sample two national parks in one trip. Visitors can walk along the bottom of the valley or hike the scenic crest of Bolinas Ridge. The Olema Valley's historic farms and fields offer pleasant roadside scenery on the way to Tomales Bay, Bolinas Lagoon, or Point Reyes.

The Valley

Springtime is the best time to see the Olema Valley in all its pastoral splendor, with the creeks babbling, the wildflowers blooming, and the grass green. Farmers have raised dairy cattle and planted apple orchards in the valley for over a century. The regal, white houses of early dairy farms stand all along Highway 1, their rooms and surrounding pastures now used by modern-day beef ranchers. Today, many of these properties belong to the National Park Service, though most have been leased back to the ranchers. Please be considerate of private ranching activities.

Samuel P. Taylor State Park

Just east of the Olema Valley is 2,600-acre Samuel P. Taylor State Park, offering trails, picnic sites, and camping facilities for cars, hikers, and bicyclists (see pp. 68-69 for more details).

Bolinas Ridge

Far from the madding crowd, Bolinas Ridge is one of GGNRA's most secluded areas. The ridge rises all along the east side of the Olema Valley. Its redwood and fir forests provided much of the lumber used to build San Francisco, transforming much of the ridge into grassland and chaparral.

Apple Orchard

Driving north on West Ridgecrest Boulevard from Mt. Tam, visitors will see an old apple orchard just before reaching the Bolinas/Fairfax Road. The orchard's slopes provide a pleasant and sheltered picnic spot.

Hagmaeir Pond

On a hot summer day, Olema Valley visitors driving north may see a lot of cars parked by the roadside, seemingly in the middle of nowhere. The cars mark the path to Hagmaeir Pond, a small, farm pond popular with sunbathers.

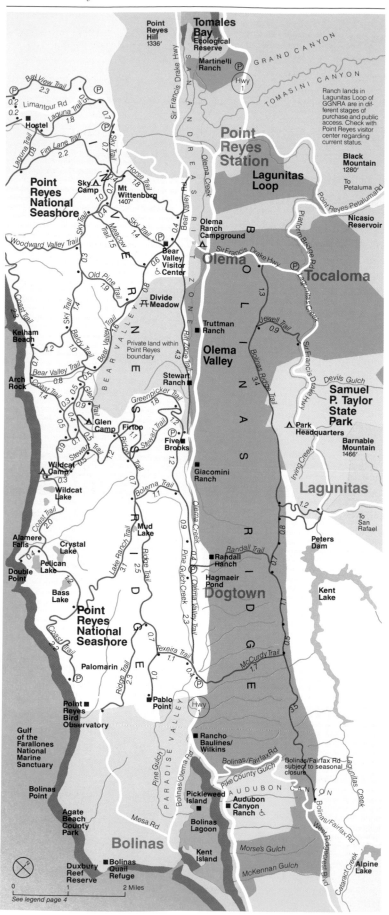

Trails

Visitors can chose from a variety of valley floor and ridge trails in the Olema Valley area. Five Brooks is the main trailhead for hikes in both GGNRA and Point Reyes National Seashore.

Olema Valley Trail

Features: Pastoral valley scenery, Morgan horses, creeks

Access: Start at the Five Brooks Trailhead. Take the Bolema Trail south to the Olema Valley Trail and continue till the trail ends at the McCurdy Trail.

One way: 4.9 miles/ moderate

Rift Zone Trail

Features: Pastoral scenery, San Andreas Fault zone features

Access: From Five Brooks Trailhead, walk north on the Amanda Way and Rift Zone Trails to the Bear Valley Visitor Center.

One way: 4.5 miles/ moderate

Inverness Ridge Trails

Features: Views over Olema Valley and Pacific coast

Access: From Five Brooks Trailhead, climb up over Inverness Ridge on the Stewart, Green-picker, or Bolema Trails to reach the wilderness areas of Point Reyes National Seashore.

One way: Unlimited/ moderate-strenuous

Bolinas Ridge Trail

Features: Spectacular vistas, mountain biking, pastures, woods

Access: Start at the junction of West Ridge-crest Boulevard and the Bolinas/Fairfax Road and hike to Sir Francis Drake Boulevard (or vice versa).

One way: 11 miles/ moderate

McCurdy/Randall Loop

Features: Manzanita, fir and redwood forests, coastal and lagoon views

Access: Start a mile north of Dogtown on Highway 1. Take the McCurdy Trail up to the Bolinas Ridge Trail, then north to the Randall Trail. Take the Randall Trail down and across Highway 1, then return via the Olema Valley Trail.

Round trip: 8 miles/ moderate

The San Andreas Fault

With the San Andreas fault slicing straight through the Olema Valley, visitors can stand on two geologic plates at one time. The west side of the valley and Point Reyes sit on the Pacific plate while the east, along with the rest of the continent, is on the North American plate. The San Andreas fault is not one crack in the earth's surface, but rather, a rift zone containing many faults and lines of geologic activity. Examples of fault topography in the Olema Valley include minor ridges parallel to Bolinas and Inverness Ridges, hollows, sag ponds, and offset drains such as Olema and Pine Gulch Creeks. These two creeks flow side by side down the valley in parallel but opposite directions. (See Earthquake Trail, p. 94, for more information about the San Andreas Fault.)

Scouring Rush

Growing along the creeks in the Olema Valley is an ancient plant species called Scouring Rush. Pioneers gave this primitive plant its unusual name when they discovered the silicon in it, which made the horsetail good for scouring pans out in the wild. Visitors need only rub one of the plant's bristly stem tops between their fingers to feel the fine grains of silicon. The plant also makes a good cure for stinging nettles.

Scouring Rush-horsetail

Historic Valley Drive

One way to visit the Olema Valley is to take a driving tour of its many historic dairy ranches and other features. Start at the south end of the valley and drive toward the town of Olema, picking out landmarks from the map along the way. The mileages given below indicate the distance from the Wilkins Ranch on Highway 1 — just beyond the 17/01 mile marker near the Bolinas/Olema Road intersection. Set the odometer!

Rancho Baulines

Rancho Baulines, Wilkins Ranch

Out in front of the gabled Wilkins Ranch, just beyond the 17/01 mile marker, is a mailbox marked #5350. Built around 1876, this white frame house with green shutters and a facade of fish-scale shingles is one of the oldest continually inhabited homes in the valley. Surrounding the home is evidence of almost a hundred years of dairying — a creamery with diamond-paned windows, a calving shed, and a rustic redwood barn built in 1866 entirely without nails.

Original Olema/Bolinas Road

Traces of the old valley road can be seen beyond Dogtown on the right, evoking the time when valley residents traveled by wagon and buggy. The original dirt grade taken by these early vehicles follows a visibly higher route along some curves. On others, the eucalyptus trees depart from the shoulder of Highway 1 to line the original road.

Cronin's Gulch

Farther along, the road passes over a nondescript ravine named in memory of a gruesome, local tragedy. The wife of Timothy Cronin mysteriously disappeared from their nearby house on August 12, 1866. During a marital squabble, Cronin murdered his wife, wrapped her in a gunny sack, and buried her. Then, he hastily built a duck pond over the burial site. Suspicious of the new duck pond, investigators examined the site and found the body. Cronin was sentenced to death.

Sarah Randall

The Randall Family

Randall Ranch

The solitary, white frame Victorian farmhouse at 4.1 miles on the right is the Randall Ranch. This old building was built by Sarah Randall, an enterprising pioneer woman of the 1800s. Soon after settling in the Olema Valley, a neighbor shot and killed Sarah's husband. Though grief-stricken, Sarah Randall went on to run their dairy ranch single-handedly with great success.

Olema Valley

Stewart Ranch

Giacomini Ranch

Next, at 5.8 miles on the right, is the Giacomini Ranch. One of the ranch's previous land-owners was James Pedrotti, the first of several Italian-Swiss dairy-men to settle here. The many-angled roof of the ranch house shows how

two separate residences were combined in the early 20th century to form a single home. In addition to the horse and dairy barns commonly seen in the Olema Valley, the property has several locally unusual features, namely a circa-1900 carriage-house and three chicken coops.

Stewart Ranch

Built in 1865, the Stewart Ranch, at 6.8 miles on the left, is the earliest surviving residence of the Olds family. According to family tradition, Nelson Olds struck a gold vein in Sierra County, enabling the family to buy 4,366 acres of the Olema Valley. The Stewart house's comfortable front veranda and hand-split, redwood-shingle roof stand amid the barns, stables, silo, and early milking facilities of this historic dairy ranch.

Truttman Ranch

Located at 8.2 miles on the left, the Truttman Ranch was deemed the most successful dairy business in the valley by a farm correspondent in 1862. "The whole arrangement of barn yards, corrals, pens for swine, domestic fowls, and all that appertains to a well-arranged farm and dairy gives evidence that what's worth doing is worth doing well." Two modern board-and-batten houses have re-placed the original home, which burned to the ground long ago. Several 19th-century barns remain however, including a wooden frame dairy with stalls for 80 cows.

Truttman Ranch

Olema Inn

At the intersection of Sir Francis Drake Boulevard and Highway 1 stands the venerable old Olema Inn, once a stagecoach stop and local saloon.

Pointers

- The Bolinas/Fairfax Road is often closed in the winter due to landslides and in the summer due to fire hazards.

- Hikers should bring water and other necessities. Olema Valley trails have few public facilities.

Information:

Ranger Station: 663-1092

Samuel P. Taylor State Park: 488-9897

Tomales Bay & GGNRA North

Canoeing
Kayaking
Sailing
Crabbing
Fishing
Windsurfing
Hiking

Tomales Bay is a sheltered, 15-mile-long, scenic estuary at the north end of the Olema Valley. One of the best ways to visit Tomales is to climb into a canoe, kayak, or sailboat and get out onto the water. Those who prefer to remain on dry land can take the scenic drive along the northeastern edge of Tomales or visit one of several coastal access points. These access points are owned and managed by a variety of agencies including GGNRA, Tomales Bay State Park, and Point Reyes National Seashore.

Martinelli Ranch

Martinelli Ranch

Visitors can enjoy a scenic hike to the edge of Tomales Bay at the Martinelli Ranch. This 259-acre ranch lies about 1.75 miles northwest from the town of Point Reyes Station on Highway 1. At the entrance on the bay side of the highway, visitors will see a sign marked "Tomales Bay Trail." From there, it's an easy, half-mile walk through open grassland and past a beautiful freshwater pond to the bayfront. A small promontory brings visitors to a viewpoint nearly 100 feet above the water, which offers dramatic bay vistas and overlooks the point where inland creeks flow into the marshy fringes of the bay. GGNRA only recently acquired the Martinelli Ranch, extending its parklands north of Olema Valley.

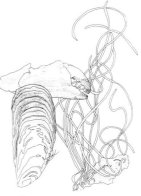

The Bay

Down in the depths of Tomales Bay live clams, oysters, crabs, fish, and a rich variety of marine life. The fish not only attract fishermen, but also natural predators such as pelicans, gulls, herons, and seals. The Bay's unusually straight narrow shape reflects the course of the San Andreas fault.

A Paddle to Hog Island

For kayak and canoeing enthusiasts, Hog Island makes a wonderful Tomales Bay trip. The best place to put in is Heart's Desire Beach on the south shore. From there, it's a peaceful paddle along the bay's interesting shoreline and beautiful beaches to the island itself, a miniature mountain of rock surrounded by bay waters.

Tomales Bay State Park

Tomales Bay State Park affords waterfront access on both sides of the bay. To the north, lies Millerton Point and Alan P. Sieroty Beach, a day-use area eight miles northwest of Point Reyes Station on Highway 1 which offers picnic spots and beach access. On the southwest side of the bay, Heart's Desire Beach is a nice spot for picnicking, camping, and warm water swimming.

Lagunitas Loop

Some of GGNRA's newest properties encompass the rural lands of the Genazzi, McFadden, and McIssac ranches, ranches which are either bordered or bisected by Lagunitas Creek. The creek, a salmon and steelhead spawning area, is the principal water course emptying into Tomales Bay. The National Park Service is still preparing public access to the loop area, which is bordered by the Point Reyes-Petaluma Road to the north and east; Sir Francis Drake Boulevard to the south; and Highway 1 to the west. Before visiting, please call for current access information.

Freshwater Shrimp

Down among the exposed roots on the banks of Lagunitas Creek lives the endangered California freshwater shrimp — the only native species of freshwater shrimp found in the state today. These tiny shrimp (1-2 inches long) feed on detritus, recycling nutrients from dead leaves and other organic floating materials. The state's entire California freshwater shrimp population inhabits fewer than ten streams, including Lagunitas Creek, in the area encompassed by Napa, Sonoma, and Marin counties.

Tomales Bay Ecological Reserve

Tomales Bay Ecological Reserve is a marshy, tidal, wildlife sanctuary — the home of many shorebirds, wading birds, and waterfowl. Visitors can gain access to this California Department of Fish and Game reserve from a big turnout on Highway 1 north of Point Reyes Station. Watch for the sign!

Curlew

Pintail Duck

Hamlet on the Bay

The old Jensen oyster farm at the north end of Tomales Bay was once the site of a railroad station identified on historic maps as Hamlet. The dairy rancher at nearby Pierce Point Ranch loaded his butter onto the railroad at Hamlet for transport to Sausalito and on to San Francisco by ferry. GGNRA recently acquired this 40-acre parcel, which offers direct access to the shoreline and views of the bay's outlet into the Pacific. The National Park Service is still developing public access to the Jensen property, so please check its current status before visiting.

Pointers

◆ There's a public boat launch at Miller Park north of Marshall on Highway 1.

◆ Those with a taste for oysters can buy these delicacies fresh from the bay at locations along Highway 1.

Information: 663-1092

Tomales Bay State Park: 669-1140

Point Reyes National Seashore

Hiking
Walking
Swimming
Camping
Picnicking
Whale watching
Visitor information

O ne of the most stunning oceanfront parks in the world is Point Reyes National Seashore — GGNRA's national park neighbor. It's a land of diverse natural features, a wilderness of beaches, bays, dunes, esteros, and forests. Though 40 miles north of San Francisco today, this famous peninsula was once located near the Tehachipi Mountains in Southern California. As the only piece of land in the region on the northward moving Pacific plate, Point Reyes is on its way to Alaska at a rate of two inches a year.

The Beaches, Bays, and Esteros

Point Reyes has every kind of shoreline area, from the wild and wind-chilled, great beaches of the northwest side to the protected areas of Drakes Bay and Limantour Spit to the south. In addition, two lush esteros wind their sinewy way to the park's southern coast.

Limantour Beach & Drake's Estero

Bear Valley Visitor Center

A good place to get acquainted with the seashore is the visitor center at Bear Valley. Apart from excellent exhibits, maps, and park information, the Bear Valley complex has a life-size copy of a Miwok Indian village, an auditorium, and a Morgan Horse ranch.

Earthquake Trail

The 0.6-mile paved Earthquake Trail begins in Bear Valley and takes visitors on an informational walk through key features of the San Andreas fault zone.

Pierce Point Ranch

Pierce Point Ranch is a restored 1860s dairy farm open for self-guided tours. One of the park's most spectacular trails leads from the ranch to the Pacific.

Point Reyes Lighthouse

Out on a great headland of the Point Reyes peninsula is a historic lighthouse. Visitors must descend 309 steps to reach the light (and climb back up again afterwards).

Wilderness Area and Trails

The southern half of the Point Reyes National Seashore is a 32,000-acre designated wilderness area with more than 70 miles of trails and several hike-in campgrounds.

Pointers

♦ Seasons are often reversed at Point Reyes, with fog and cold in the summer and clear days in the winter.

♦ For more information, pick up a copy of Wilderness Press' excellent pictorial landform map of Point Reyes National Seashore and the San Andreas fault.

Information:
663-1092

Quick Glance Index

The following list credits those illustrators, photographers, and organizations whose graphics appear in this publication.

Please note that explanations are made in parentheses only when there is more than one photo or illustration on the page.

Color Photos

Janet Delaney
pp. 6, 24, 26, 29, 36, 40, 47, 49

Roy Eisenhardt
Front cover (Alcatraz), pp. 15, 57

Richard Frear,
National Park Service
pp. 9, 23, 28, 52-53, 63, 66, 77, 81, Back cover (Muir Woods, Fort Point)

Dr. John Hafernik
Front cover (Mission Blue Butterfly)

Randy Hogue
p. 78

Mindy Manville
Front Cover (Golden Gate Bridge, ranger), pp. 2, 10, Back cover (poppy)

James M. Morley
p. 75, Back cover (Pt. Bonita Lighthouse)

Baron Wolman
pp. 35, 83, 84, 91, 94

Black & White Photos

Bancroft Library
pp. 33, 90 (Randall family & home)

California Academy of Sciences, Picture Collection, Hogue & Associates
p. 85

Janet Delaney
pp. 9, 13, 25 (marina), 38 (beach today), 40, 48 (horse), 66, 67, 87

The Exploratorium
p. 25 (palace)

Fort Point & Army Museum Association
pp. 31 (barracks & horse patrol), 32 (guns), 60 (Baker), 61 (Spencer)

Fraenkel Gallery
p. 45 (casino)

Richard Frear,
National Park Service
pp. 7 (woods & bridge), 20 (Thayer), 24 (piers), 39 (beach), 42 (seals), 45 (today), 49, 56 (cove), 64

Golden Gate Bridge Highway & Transportation District
p. 34 (Strauss)

Randy Hogue
p. 80

Nancy Hornor
p. 31 (creek)

Mindy Manville
p. 86

John Martini
p. 60 (Townsley)

Robert J. Martini
p. 41 (ship)

James M. Morley
p. 79

National Maritime Museum
pp. 19, 21 (Balclutha & Wapama), 39 (junk), 47, 82

S.F. History Room, S.F. Library
p. 34 (Fremont)

Ted Tuescher
p. 79 (Tam)

Wildlife Center
p. 8 (bobcat)

Photos not credited above are from National Park Service collections in the GGNRA.

Illustrations

California Academy of Sciences, Picture Collection
pp. 3, 7 (shipwreck), 8 (SF), 17 (heron), 27 (crab), 33, 39 (fishermen), 43 (tansy), 62 (pelican), 65 (paintbrush, grass, buttercup & zigadene), 66 (eucalyptus & birds), 67 (elk), 68, 69 (fire), 74 (branch & deer), 81 (Monarch), 83 (anemone & seaslug), 87 (logs & hay), 89 (horsetail), 93 (duck)

Pedro Gonzalez
p. 58 (hawk head)

Pieter Folkens
pp. 44 (sea lions), 82 (whales), 86 (seals)

Fort Mason Center
p. 8 (masks), 22 (masks & artist)

Jim Hahn
p. 6 (lighthouse)

Craig Hannah
pp. 17 (gull), 70

Elise Hillend
pp. 51 (snake), 93 (shrimp)

Kevin Metcalf
Front cover (pelican, whale, redwood tree), Back cover (hawk, bobcat paw print, nudibranch)

Nevada Dept. of Wildlife, *Nevada Raptors*
p. 58 (silhouettes)

Paul Okamoto
pp. 90, 91 (buildings)

Ricardo Perez
pp. 63 (heron), 65 (poppy), 92 (oyster)

Reineck & Reineck
pp. 22, 80, 89 (diagrams); Spot illustrations throughout

Ane Rovetta
pp. 7 (sea lions), 27 (bear), 64, 74 (chipmunk), 78 (raccoon), 85 (egret), 86 (worm)

David Sibley,
Cape May Bird Observatory
pp. 50 (Cooper's Hawk), 58 (Large Sharp-shinned Hawk)

Society of California Pioneers
p. 38 (water carrier)

Stanford University Press
Reprinted from *Illustrated Flora of the Pacific States*, 4 volumes, by LeRoy Abrams and Roxana Stinchfield Ferris with the permission of the publishers. © 1960 by the Board of Trustees of the Leland Stanford Junior University.
pp. 6 (rose), 41, 49 (flowers), 65 (iris, milkmaid & redmaid), 66 (willow),

University of California Press
Shore Wildflowers of California, Oregon & Washington by Phillip Munz, 1964.
pp. 65 (sun cup), 74 (flower), 81 (grass)

Text

Quotes appearing in the following two sections of the guide were reprinted with permission as listed below.

A Visit from the HMS Racoon:
Excerpted from *The Voyage of the Racoon*, courtesy of the Book Club of California, ©1958.
p. 27

Adolph Sutro — Mayor, Millionaire, Philanthropist.
Reprinted with the permission of the *S.F. Examiner*.
p. 44

Production Notes

Copyediting
Anne B. McDonald

Typesetting
Book designed using Apple Macintosh II with Quark Express 2.0A.

Color Separations
Maps: Solzer & Hail Inc.
Book: Colorprep Inc.

Printing
Fong & Fong Printers & Lithographers